Sir Winston Churchill

MEN AND EVENTS

General Editor: A. F. Alington, M.A.
Lately H.M. Staff Inspector, Ministry of Education

*

THE BATTLE OF BRITAIN
by N. D. Smith

THE ENGLISH CIVIL WAR
by Sutherland Ross

THE LAMPS GO OUT
1914 and the Outbreak of War
by A. F. Alington

SIR WINSTON CHURCHILL
by Alan Farrell

THE MAN WHO FREED THE SLAVES
The Story of William Wilberforce
by A. and H. B. Lawson

(*further titles are in preparation*)

Sir Winston Churchill

by

ALAN FARRELL

FABER AND FABER

24 Russell Square

London

First published in mcmlxii
by Faber and Faber Limited
24 Russell Square London W.C.1
Printed in Great Britain by
Latimer Trend & Co Ltd Plymouth

For Margaret and Peter

Acknowledgments

The author is indebted to the following for permission to reproduce copyright material from the speeches and writings of Sir Winston Churchill: Cassell & Co. Ltd., and McClelland & Stewart Ltd. of Toronto, for material from *Into Battle* and *The Unrelenting Struggle*; Cassell & Co. Ltd., and the Houghton Mifflin Co. of Boston, Mass., for material from *The Sinews of Peace* and *The Second World War*; and Odhams Press Ltd. for material from *My Early Life* and *Thoughts and Adventures*.

He is grateful to the following for permission to reproduce copyright photographs: The Radio Times Hulton Picture Library for the illustrations numbered 1a, 1b and 2b; and the Imperial War Museum for the illustrations numbered 2a, 3a, 3b and 4.

Contents

CONTENTS

Illustrations

CHAPTER I

'The Happiest Days of One's Life'

When the English monarchy was restored in 1660, King Charles II conferred a knighthood on a writer, soldier and Member of Parliament named Winston Churchill, who had been a Royalist in the Civil War. John, the third son of this first Sir Winston Churchill, was an even greater soldier, probably the greatest in the history of this country, for he led the resistance of Europe against Louis XIV of France, who, like Hitler some 250 years later, dreamed of ruling the whole continent. Queen Anne made John Churchill Duke of Marlborough for his services, and after his great victory of Blenheim in 1704, gave him land and money to build a home fit for a national hero and the saviour of Europe. It was in this great palace of Blenheim, in the lovely Oxfordshire village of Woodstock, that Marlborough's descendant Winston Leonard Spencer Churchill was born on 30th November 1874.

Winston's father, Lord Randolph Churchill, had been elected Member of Parliament for Woodstock during the same year, and was later to become Secretary of State for India and Chancellor of the Exchequer. He was as dashing and brilliant a figure in Parliament as he was at the balls and receptions of the nobility. Lady Randolph, the gay,

beautiful and popular daughter of an American business-
man, not only adorned these social occasions, but helped
her husband to fight his political battles. Winston himself
as a young child was a sturdy red-head with a round,
freckled face and a blunt nose, rather awed and frightened
by the splendour of his parents, who, like most aristo-
crats of the last century, spent very little time with their
children. It was lucky for Winston that his nurse, Mrs.
Everest, was a loving and motherly woman.

When he was seven, Winston was sent to a preparatory
school near Ascot, where the headmaster, a severe and
humourless man, beat his pupils until they bled. Winston
suffered as much as any, but, far from allowing his spirit
to be broken, he once paid back a beating by kicking the
headmaster's straw hat to pieces! His health was affected,
however, and after a serious attack of pneumonia he was
sent to another school at Brighton. There the kindly
maiden ladies in charge allowed him to spend his time on
English, French and history, subjects that delighted him.
He also read adventure books, took healthy exercise, and
earned from one of the mistresses the title of 'the
naughtiest small boy in the world'.

Winston took the entrance examination for Harrow at
the age of thirteen. The great public school on the hill was
judged to be healthier for a boy with a weak chest than
Eton, close to the Thames and its mists, where most of
the Churchills had gone to school. Latin was more important in the public schools of seventy years ago than it
is now—and Winston had stoutly resisted all Latin
teaching at Ascot and Brighton. When his Latin paper
for that entrance examination was collected at the end of
two hours, it had on it a figure 1 in brackets, a blot and
some smudges! Nevertheless, Winston was accepted, as
the lowest boy in the lowest form. Perhaps the head-

master felt sure that a son of Lord Randolph must have abilities that did not come to the surface in examinations. A year later, when he had proved that he could, or would, never understand Latin, he was transferred to the 'modern side'. It was lucky that he was taught English and Mathematics by inspired and sympathetic masters, since he stubbornly refused to learn anything that did not interest him, or to work for any master he disliked.

During his time at Harrow Winston broke nearly every school rule; among other irregularities, he kept dogs in a house in the town, and exercised them in the company of a townsman. There is even a story that once, when the headmaster told Winston that he was gravely displeased with him, he retorted, 'And I, sir, have very grave reason to be displeased with you!'

One day in his first term, Winston noticed a boy of about his own size day-dreaming at the very edge of the 'Ducker', as the school swimming pool was called. He crept up behind and pushed, considerately holding on to the other boy's towel. Within seconds his victim, un-expectedly muscular and powerful, had heaved himself out of the water and flung the surprised Winston far into the pool. Horrified bystanders hastened to explain to the new boy, as he climbed out, that his victim was Leo Amery, Sixth-Former, House Captain and champion of gymnastics! Winston went to apologize. He had mis-taken Amery for a Fourth-Former, he explained, because he was so small. The other's expression must have shown at once that this was not the most tactful excuse, for Winston babbled hastily that his own father, who was a great man, was small too. Amery laughed good-naturedly, and accepted the clumsy apology.

The son of the spectacular Lord Randolph and des-cendant of the incomparable Marlborough was preoccupied with greatness even at this early age. Once when he was beaten by another senior boy, he retorted, 'I shall be a greater man than you!' The senior, destined to become a mere bishop, understandably mistook this prophecy for impudence, and gave Winston two more strokes.

Although he may not have realized it then, Winston was simply a rebel against the public school system. He hated organized team games. He respected those who earned his respect, and not those who happened to be in authority over him. He was not much liked by the other boys, but did not seem to care for popularity. When he brought his beloved old nurse, Mrs. Everest, to Harrow, showed her round the school and took her along the High Street on his arm, he did not notice that the whole school was buzzing with the news.

Yet even at Harrow there were some triumphs. He won a prize in his first term for reciting twelve hundred lines of Macaulay's *Lays* (with his powerful memory he could often correct his masters when they misquoted—and he often did!). He could compose correct and flowing verse. He won the Public Schools Fencing Competition, and he swam for his House.

Much later Winston said that his schooldays discouraged him, and that if he could relive his boyhood he would not choose to go to a public school again. At another time he declared himself in favour of the public school system. Perhaps he believes that it has a great deal to offer most boys, but that the few strong and remarkable characters like himself must become very hard square pegs when they are forced into uncomfortably round holes. Two incidents towards the end of his unpromising school career helped to guide him in directions in which his unusual qualities were to be allowed to develop more freely.

When Winston was deploying and manœuvring his magnificent collection of 1,500 model soldiers during a school holiday, his father, having studied the scene thoughtfully for some time, asked him if he would like to go into the army. Winston was delighted, and one of the most important decisions of his life was promptly taken.

While he was staying with his aunt at Bournemouth, he was playing a game with his brother and a young cousin on the estate when he found himself at bay on a rustic bridge that spanned a small ravine full of young firs, with a pursuer approaching from each end. Daring and impulsive as always, he jumped off the bridge, hoping that the fir branches would act as a safety net. They did nothing to cushion his fall, and he crashed twenty-nine feet to the ground, rupturing a kidney. He was unconscious for three days, and an invalid for almost a year.

Winston and his parents lived in London with his grandmother, the Dowager Duchess of Marlborough, during his convalescence, and he was able to meet and talk with the great statesmen of the time, and to listen intently to debates in the House of Commons. He has always had an appetite for contest of any kind, with no quarter given or asked, and the ferocious exchanges of the Victorian Parliament fascinated him. At this time, too, he talked more often with his father and began to feel less shy in his company. They might have become closer and more friendly still in time, but there was very little time left. Lord Randolph was already suffering terribly from the illness from which he was to die less than two years later.

Having scraped through the entrance examination for Sandhurst at the third attempt, Winston found himself at last studying subjects and practising skills the value of which he could understand—military tactics and engineering, army law, organization and administration, the demolition of bridges with explosives, reconnaissance. Besides, he was a cavalry cadet, and as he loved horses and riding, much of his work was sheer delight. He spent his leaves from Sandhurst in point-to-point racing and steeplechasing.

The serious accident and long illness at the end of his schooldays had helped to mature Winston just before he started his professional training. The end of his time at Sandhurst and the beginning of his military career were marked by deeper distresses which emphasized brutally the end of boyhood and dependence.

Two months after his twentieth birthday, and two months before he was commissioned, his father died. Lord Randolph had been for Winston a distant, Olympian hero. But the son now remembered moments when his father had tried to break down the barrier between them. Once when Winston had fired at a rabbit on the lawn under his father's window, Lord Randolph had scolded him harshly, then relented and talked to him in the friendliest way, explaining that worries made older people inconsiderate towards their children, and asking him to make allowances. In later life Winston was to long for the power to put time in reverse and talk with his father as one mature man to another.

Lord Randolph's death was the occasion of sudden, important decisions for Winston. He was about to embark on a career of responsibility and considerable expense, for no cavalry officer was expected to live on his army pay. He must not remain dependent upon his mother's generosity, but must make a second, and profitable, career for himself.

Six months later, his childhood nurse, Mrs. Everest, died. At his father's funeral Winston had been the grave, responsible and efficient head of an aristocratic family; by Mrs. Everest's grave he wept freely and openly. In the great Victorian household in which public life kept both parents away from their children, the old nurse had been his closest friend and confidante.

CHAPTER II

Subaltern and War Correspondent: Looking for Trouble in a Peaceful World

The young officers of the 4th Queen's Own Hussars were elegant, languid, pleasant companions, rich enough not to worry about their absurd pay of fourteen shillings a day. Their duties were so light that the five months' annual leave which they spent in hunting and the delights of the London season was probably the most exhausting part of their routine. Their new fellow-officer, not for the first time, found himself a square peg in a round hole. While his companions talked smoothly on topics so unimportant that it was hard to disagree with them, Churchill argued and lectured and made himself unpopular. When they were looking forward to two and a half months' hunting, he was arranging to spend his leave in the one place in that peaceful nineteenth-century world where a soldier could see fighting.

For years the Spanish Government had been waging war on rebel bands in the jungles of Cuba. Through the British ambassador in Madrid, a close friend of his late father, Churchill arranged to attach himself to the

Spanish forces, and in November 1895, he sailed with a fellow-officer, Reginald Barnes, for the Caribbean.

This move alone would have shown that Churchill was blessed with the more initiative and high spirits than most of his fellows; but, even more resourcefully, he arranged to send descriptions of his adventures to the *Daily Graphic* at £5 an article. In future whenever he embarked on an adventure he made certain that his talent for describing thrilling experiences would bring him a profit.

The government troops in Cuba had very little idea of how to deal with the guerrillas, who gathered suddenly, attacked from front or rear or flank without warning, dispersed as suddenly and retired. The Spanish had immovable defence lines and strongpoints, within which a small number of very large columns of troops in conspicuous white uniforms marched rigidly through the dense jungle, like sluggish caterpillars at the mercy of ants. It was a good lesson for keen young officers on the danger of clinging to out-of-date methods of warfare. It also gave them a chance to see how they themselves behaved under fire.

Churchill and Barnes joined a four-thousand strong Spanish column in the fever-ridden town of Sancti Spiritus. After days of riding through moist, luxuriant jungle, the two Englishmen came under fire for the first time. As Churchill was eating his breakfast, a horse just behind him was shot. The following day they were fired on while dressing after a swim. That night Churchill heard bullets zipping through the thatch of their hut, and wondered whether the Spanish officer in the next hammock was fat enough to provide cover from fire! Something like a pitched battle was fought the following day. Churchill and the Spanish officers, on horseback behind the lines, watched the government troops drive the rebels from their positions and into the jungle, where they were safe from pursuit. That was the end of the campaign for Churchill and Barnes, for they left for home the next day.

Churchill returned from Cuba with the Spanish Military Medal, a taste for rum cocktails and Havana cigars, and the habit of the *siesta*, which enabled him to work with unflagging energy into the small hours of the morning during the Second World War when younger men around him were almost exhausted. More important, he had learned that military commanders must be always ready to change their strategy and tactics to meet those of the enemy, and he had embarked on a profitable career as a war correspondent.

On reaching home, Churchill and Barnes found that their regiment was to sail to India the following autumn. This allowed them six months of gaiety in the brilliant summer of 1896. Churchill met Sir Bindon Blood, Commander-in-Chief on the North-west Frontier of India, during this time, and extracted from him a promise that he would let him join a frontier expedition if trouble should break out with the tribesmen.

As soon as the troopship dropped anchor at Bombay, a group of eager officers hired a small boat to get ashore. Churchill, the most eager of all, grabbed for an iron ring fixed to the quay, and an unlucky movement of the boat dislocated his right shoulder. He had to take precautions against fresh dislocations for the rest of his life.

The 4th Hussars were stationed in the southern Indian town of Bangalore, a beautiful place with an ideal climate. Churchill lived with the three other officers in a pink-and-white bungalow with purple bougainvillea twining round its pillars. After mornings spent on parades and other duties, prolonged siestas prepared them for polo in the evenings. But Churchill in India was no more content to accept the leisured life of the cavalry officer than he had been at Aldershot; he wrote to his mother asking her to send him books, and when the monthly packages began to arrive, he devoted hours each day to the study of science, philosophy, politics and history. His best-loved works were Gibbon's *Decline and Fall of the Roman Empire* and Macaulay's *History of England*, which he read more than once, learning his favourite passages by heart. Churchill has always preferred books about action and the exercise of power; indeed, thought, for him, is worthwhile only if it leads to action. He read philosophy at this time simply because he wanted to equip himself with the general culture that he believed he would need for his future greatness.

His impatience with garrison life showed itself in other ways. He irritated those around him, as he had done in Aldershot and London, by his cocksure arguments. Invited to dinner by Lord Sandhurst, this twenty-two-year-old subaltern overwhelmed his host with opinions, and even advice, on British and Indian affairs. Lord Sandhurst was Governor of Bombay!

Besides talking, Churchill was incessantly looking for any chance of adventure. He heard, while on home leave in the summer of 1897, that Sir Bindon Blood was to lead an expedition against warring North-west-Frontier tribesmen, and promptly sent the general a telegram reminding him of his promise of the previous year. A reply awaited him at Bombay on his return to India. Blood had no vacancy for a regimental officer, but could perhaps find room for him as a newspaper correspondent. The *Pioneer*, an English-language newspaper in Allahabad, agreed to employ him, and he arranged through his mother to send reports at £5 a column to the *Daily Telegraph*.

On 16th September 1897, he accompanied a brigade of Sir Bindon's forces which penetrated into the Mamund Valley, about fifty miles north of Peshawar, to destroy the villages of the fierce Mamunds as a punishment for rebellion. The keen-eyed tribesmen looked down from the hills, and saw the cavalry dismount at a village and open fire. Churchill accompanied a party of about fifteen which was ordered to give covering fire while a party of eighty-five Sikhs and four officers withdrew from the position. It was this weak detachment that first saw the gleam of swords and the puffs of rifle smoke among the rocks ahead as the tribesmen prepared to attack.

The two sides were soon locked in hand-to-hand fighting. Casualties quickly mounted in Churchill's small party. A tribesman who had slashed a wounded officer with his sword flung a stone at Churchill as a challenge. Churchill replied with revolver fire, then, finding himself completely isolated from his own troops, dashed for cover. After some hours' fighting, Churchill's party withdrew, carrying their wounded with them.

Churchill was posted later to the 31st Punjab Infantry, which had suffered many officer casualties, and saw action in a number of affrays before the campaign ended. Sir Bindon mentioned him in despatches as 'having made himself useful at a critical moment'.

Reluctant to rejoin his regiment in peaceful Bangalore, Churchill used every effort to get himself attached to an expedition against the formidable Afridis of Tirah, elsewhere on the Frontier; but he had made enemies by criticizing glaring mistakes in the conduct of the previous expedition in his newspaper articles. Besides, his fellow-officers of the 4th Hussars were growing impatient. So he returned to his southern garrison, where he worked for three or four hours a day on *The Story of the Malakand Field Force, 1897.*

This first book was a great success, and was read by the Prime Minister, Lord Salisbury, and the Prince of Wales. The two months of furious writing had earned him as much as his lieutenant's pay brought him in two years. He returned to writing with renewed zest, and produced his only work of fiction.

Savrola is a very youthful and violent, even bloodthirsty romance, but no one interested in the author can be bored by his hero; for Savrola, though a bitter opponent of Socialism, overthrows a Fascist tyrant; he is not only a fearless man of action, but also a wide reader of Macaulay, and his fiery passion as an orator hides the secret that his every sentence has been weighed, forged and polished with the utmost care before it is uttered. Whatever its faults, *Savrola* was well received when it was published in serial form, and the £700 it earned meant a further step towards independence for a hard-pressed young cavalry officer.

When the prospect of boring garrison duty, relieved only by writing, seemed to stretch indefinitely into the future, Churchill's keen nose scented adventure far from Bangalore.

In the Sudan, ruled by Britain and Egypt, but with its own monarch, the Khedive, there had been a rebellion of the fanatical sect of Dervishes, and the Anglo-Egyptian forces had been defeated. The rebels had captured Khartoum and killed its defender, General Gordon. Government troops had been pulled out, and the Dervishes had established an insupportable tyranny. Sixteen years later, in the spring of 1898, General Kitchener, commander-in-chief of the Anglo-Egyptian army, launched a campaign to liberate the Sudan.

Once again the hard-hitting criticisms in Churchill's *Malakand* book stood in the way of a posting. Senior officers were unwilling to have him under their command. The mighty Kitchener himself, approached by Lady Randolph, and even by the Prime Minister, remained adamant.

Then somehow Churchill discovered that the Adjutant-General to the Forces, Sir Evelyn Wood, was annoyed that Kitchener had interfered with the posting of officers, which was the Adjutant-General's responsibility. He asked Sir Evelyn for a posting to Kitchener's command, and Sir Evelyn, glad of a chance to score a point in the dispute, attached him to the 21st Lancers, on condition that he paid his own expenses and that no compensation or pension should be paid to him if he became a casualty. Churchill was satisfied, for he had a contract to cover the campaign for the *Morning Post* at £15 an article.

He reached Cairo on 1st August, after the Lancers had begun the journey to the Sudan. The troop he was to command had already left, with a Lieutenant Grenfell in charge. On 1st September, after a gruelling fourteen-hundred-mile journey, Churchill, in command of a re-connaissance patrol, was the first to sight the Dervish forces near Omdurman, and was sent back to give the news to Kitchener in person. He was never easily intimidated, but he must have felt qualms at the prospect of approaching the forbidding commander-in-chief whose wishes he had defied. Fortunately Kitchener heard his report without recognizing him.

The following morning twenty thousand British troops advanced to meet sixty thousand screaming, yelling Dervishes who believed that God had already accorded them victory, and that those who were killed would be rewarded in Paradise. The British, however, were well armed and supported by artillery, while their adversaries had only out-of-date rifles, lances, swords and knives.

When first the artillery and then the rifles had wrought frightful casualties among the Dervishes, the four hundred men and horses of the 21st Lancers were ordered to charge through the scattered remnants towards Omdurman. To their complete surprise they galloped into a dry river-bed in which two or three thousand Dervishes were lying hidden, and were immediately involved in bloody hand-to-hand fighting. Churchill was leading the second troop from the right. The two right-hand troops were able to sweep round the enemy flank, since the British front was wider.

Churchill, unable to wield sword or lance effectively because of his weak shoulder, went in with a Mauser pistol. A wounded Dervish reached up from the ground to hamstring his horse with a swordstroke, but Churchill shot him dead. Another barred his path with a raised sword. This time Churchill struck the Dervish with his Mauser as he raised it to fire, and as his opponent went down, he shot his way onwards to rejoin his troop. Characteristically, as they reassembled, he asked one of his sergeants if he had enjoyed himself!

Twenty Lancers were killed and fifty wounded, and one hundred and twenty horses were lost, against only thirty or forty Dervish casualties, in this costly action. Grenfell, who had taken command of the troop designated for Churchill at Cairo, was among the dead. Omdurman was the last battle in history in which mounted swordsmen moved forward in close order on a broad front, first trotting and then galloping in obedience to bugle calls, against an enemy drawn up in ranks to bar their way.

Churchill started work on *The River War*, a history of the Sudan campaign, on the boat to England, feeling confident now that he could make his way in journalism and authorship. He had a last military duty to perform, however, before resigning his commission. He had to help his regiment to win the inter-regimental polo championship of India. In the final, Churchill was marking a back who was later to become an international—and a few days before the match he had strained the muscles of his weak shoulder. Yet the Hussars became champions by four goals to three, and Churchill scored three of the goals. He left the 4th Hussars and the army on a wave of popularity.

In the summer of 1899, Churchill's glorious political career began with a defeat. He stood as Conservative candidate for Oldham, but was unsuccessful. This was no disgrace for a Conservative newcomer to a Lancashire working-class town, but to the ambitious young ex-officer it was a setback, and it was not easy to see the next step. Fate, however, as so often before and since, obligingly showed it to him.

CHAPTER III

Adventure in South Africa:
the First Taste of Fame

Nowadays most people agree that Britain's war against the Dutch farmers, or Boers, of South Africa was stupid, greedy, and unnecessary. Its one good result, an accidental one, was the drawing together of a number of states into the Union of South Africa ten years later.

After nearly two centuries of high-handed treatment by the British, the Boers in the Transvaal had won independence in 1881. But in 1886 the discovery of diamonds near Johannesburg in the centre of the Transvaal lured hordes of adventurers, with British backing, to challenge the Boers and their Government. British troops were sent to provoke frontier incidents until the Boers were stung to retaliation, and the Boer War began.

The *Morning Post*, needing a lively and courageous war correspondent in South Africa, knew whom to call on. On 11th October 1898, Winston Churchill sailed in the same boat as the commander-in-chief, Sir Redvers Buller, with a £250-a-month contract and all expenses paid.

Everyone aboard was sure that the peaceful, slow-thinking Boers would offer only the feeblest resistance. Churchill's one fear was that the war would be over before they disembarked. His plan was to travel by rail from Cape Town to Durban and thence to Ladysmith, but he got as far as Estcourt to find that the despised Boers had surrounded Ladysmith and were threatening Southern Natal. They had gained a resounding victory at Nicholson's Nek, and were besieging Mafeking and Kimberley.

For officers, the tight little nineteenth-century British Army was almost an exclusive club; at Pietermaritzburg Churchill met his old friend and fellow-adventurer Reginald Barnes, in hospital with a bullet wound in the thigh; in Estcourt he came upon Leopold Amery, whom he had pushed into the swimming bath at Harrow, and a Captain Haldane, through whom he had tried to secure a posting to the Tirah expedition on the North-west Frontier.

Reconnaissance patrols were sent out from Estcourt in an armoured train, a laughable contraption consisting of a locomotive and tender with three iron wagons forward and two more aft, protected by thin steel sheets that let in the bullets, and by a naval six-pounder. It trundled along the sixteen miles of track left by the advancing Boers, in the certainty of being derailed and ambushed sooner or later.

Haldane was given command of an armoured-train reconnaissance patrol, and invited Churchill to accompany him. They had travelled fourteen miles, and had started back, when Boer artillery and a machine-gun engaged them on a downward slope. The engine driver decided to drive through the hail at full steam, but a thoughtfully-placed rock derailed the leading trucks, leaving the last of the three spreadeagled across the track in front of the engine.

Haldane's patrol and their six-pounder in the rear trucks held off the enemy while Churchill, with the locomotive, directed bulldozing operations to clear the track. The driver was struck in the head by a shell fragment, but Churchill rallied him with the old superstition that no one is ever hit twice in the same day. With bullets and shells whining and twittering all round them, the civilian war correspondent persuaded the soldiers he was commanding to keep their heads.

At last the track was clear, and Churchill was able to pack the wounded, now about forty, into the cab and tender. The engine then started off at walking pace, giving cover to the rest of the men from the three derailed trucks, who walked beside it. Unfortunately the locomotive began to leave the marchers behind, so Churchill jumped down from the cab and went back towards them.

Two men were coming along the cutting to meet him. Too late Churchill noticed their civilian clothes. They were Boers! With bullets whistling about his ears, he pressed himself against the side of the cutting, but it gave him no cover. After a jinking run down the railway line he succeeded in climbing out of this death-trap—only to find himself face to face with a mounted Boer brandishing a rifle. He felt for his pistol. He had left it in the cab of the locomotive. There was nothing for it but to raise his hands. He had the satisfaction of knowing that his trainload of wounded were on their way back to Estcourt, but Haldane and the rest were prisoners like himself—with the important difference that he was a civilian, and therefore liable to be executed for his part in the action.

After a sixty-mile march in torrential rain, the prisoners were herded into a train which took them to Pretoria, the capital of the Transvaal. Churchill's future looked even less bright when he was made to stand at a distance from the other prisoners; but his captors, far from bearing him any ill will, were thrilled to have the son of a lord as a prisoner. When he was sure that the part he had played in the armoured-train battle was not going to endanger his life, Churchill impudently asked to be released as a civilian war correspondent. The Natal newspapers, however, had heard the full story of the incident from the men who had returned from the ambush, and were full of praise for his soldierly conduct.

In the State Model schools, where the prisoners were guarded by ten armed policemen at a time and encircled by a ten-foot corrugated-iron fence, the monotony of captivity began. But not all the inmates intended to wait patiently for release.

Captain Haldane and a Lieutenant Brockie swiftly evolved a plan of escape. There was a circular latrine close to the fence, from which the sentry's movements could be watched. The plan was to visit the latrine before the evening meal with a number of other officers, to wait inside until the sentry was satisfied that all had left and that he could safely stroll away to chat with a fellow-sentry at a distance, then heave themselves up to the seven-foot-high latrine roof, and from there over the fence.

As soon as Churchill heard of this plan, he prevailed on the others to let him join them. On the evening of 11th December an attempt was made, in which only the sentry failed to play his part, staying close to the latrine. The next evening, when both sentries were at a distance of fifteen yards, Churchill was first over the fence, and dropped safely into a garden. He waited for half an hour in the shrubbery, dressed in a civilian suit and a Dutch parson's hat. Then a voice from the other side of the fence told him that the sentry was suspicious, and that the others could not follow.

Churchill was free, but in an unknown city, without map or compass, and the nearest neutral territory, Portuguese East Africa, was three hundred miles to the east. He had £75 and four slabs of chocolate. Walking out of the garden within five yards of a sentry, and through the suburbs of Pretoria, he found a railway line going east, and followed it for some hours, giving guarded bridges a wide berth.

An eastbound goods train clattered past. He leaped for the couplings and hoisted himself into a truck. Before it was light, he left the train and hid in a wood for the whole day, hoping to 'jump' another train after nightfall. But no train came, and he was compelled to plod along wearily, skirting bridges and wayside halts.

He was utterly exhausted, and ready to ask for help from any source, when he saw lights in the distance which he supposed to come from a native village. As he drew near, he saw that the building was a house attached to a coal mine. He knocked at the door.

'Wie's daar (Who's there)?' came the wary question in Afrikaans, the language of the Boers, from an upstairs window.

Churchill answered in English. Then the door opened, and a pale, moustached face eyed him from behind a revolver. Churchill tried to pretend that he was a Boer soldier, and talked about a train accident, but when the householder replied in perfect English, he resigned himself to telling the truth, hoping that his amazing luck would not fail him. It did not. He had called at the only English house within twenty miles! His host, John Howard, was an English settler who had become a naturalized Boer and had been allowed to continue his work as manager of the coal mine. He revealed now that Churchill's hunters had already called at the house.

With Howard in the house was a Mr. Dewsnap, an engineer from Oldham. After a huge meal the fugitive

followed Dewsnap into some disused workings of the
mine where he could stay undiscovered by the native
miners. For three days Churchill was in solitary confine-
ment—solitary, that is, except for a colony of gigantic
white rats with an appetite for candles. Then, when his
hosts judged it was safe for him to leave, he was taken to
a wayside halt and put aboard a truck loaded with bales of
wool bound for Lourenço Marques, capital of Portuguese
East Africa.

It was a two-and-a-half-day journey, but wool is a com-
fortable cargo to stow away in, and the admirable
Howard had provided plenty of good food. When he was
sure he was in Portuguese territory, he climbed on to the
tarpaulin and sang a song of triumph accompanied by
shots from his revolver.

The same afternoon, at the British Consulate in Lourenço Marques, his dirty, ill-dressed unshaven condition
caused eyebrows to lift, but when he explained who he
was, he was given a hot bath, new clothes and food, and
the news that his escape had provided headlines for the
newspapers of Europe and Africa. The Boers had issued
a poster showing a photograph of Churchill in cavalry
uniform, with a description and an offer of £25 for his
capture dead or alive.

He arrived by boat in Durban a few days later to re-
ceive a hero's welcome. Amid waving flags and blaring
bands he was chaired to the town hall, where he gave
the wildly cheering crowd the speech they clamoured
for.

The commander-in-chief, who had shown no eagerness
to meet the *Morning Post* correspondent when they sailed
to South Africa together in the *Dunottar Castle*, now
asked him to state his wishes. The answer was prompt.
Churchill wanted a commission. Buller reminded him of

the new rule that serving officers could not act as newspaper correspondents, a rule made because of Churchill's own criticisms of army commanders in despatches from India and Egypt. However, he offered him a commission in the South African Light Horse, without pay.

The British Government was now awake to the slowness and incompetence of her senior officers in South Africa, including Sir Redvers Buller himself. Churchill was present at the disastrous battle of Spion Kop, where Buller's troops, having captured a totally exposed hill, remained on its crest for a whole day under murderous shellfire, unable to advance and vainly awaiting the order to retreat, until more than 1,800 men were lost. Field-Marshal Lord Roberts, an experienced commander from the North-west Frontier, was already on his way out to replace Buller, with the ruthlessly efficient Kitchener as his Chief of Staff.

In January, February and March Roberts won a series of resounding victories which allowed Buller to relieve Ladysmith. Churchill was among the first to enter the town. After Ladysmith, with a true journalist's flair for 'copy', he joined Lord Roberts's command for the push to Johannesburg and Pretoria.

Once, in a cavalry engagement, his horse's girth snapped while he was under heavy fire, and he escaped only by leaping on to a wounded horse behind its rider. At another time he was with troops approaching Johannesburg from the west while the commander-in-chief was coming in from the east. The day before the attack, needing to reach Roberts's headquarters to send off his articles to his newspaper, he took the shortest way— through the enemy-held city with a bicycle, unnoticed by the Boers he passed in the streets! He was with the leading cavalry again at the relief of Pretoria, and had the keen pleasure of freeing his sometime fellow-prisoners from their camp.

Many people thought that the capture of Pretoria meant the end of serious fighting in South Africa, though in fact the war was to drag on for two more years. Churchill resigned his commission and returned to London to find the people delirious with excitement at the news of the relief of Mafeking.

For long afterwards Englishmen used a new word, 'mafficking' to describe wildly joyful merrymaking. Singing and dancing in the streets were new experiences for the sober, respectable subjects of Queen Victoria; but the old queen's reign was nearly over, and important changes were soon to come in the Englishman's ways of living and thinking.

Churchill, born in a great ducal palace into an aristocratic family, educated at a great public school, an ex-cavalry subaltern tested in action on the romantic Northwest Frontier, foremost in the last classic cavalry charge in history, and the representative of a staid London paper during the last great imperialist campaign, was to become a politician and statesman, and to be in the forefront of the new era. He was soon to sponsor reforms and to give his blessing to new ideas, while remaining in many ways obstinately a man of the nineteenth century.

CHAPTER IV

Lord Randolph's Son
on the Back Bench

On his return from South Africa, Churchill went to Oldham to stand again as Conservative candidate in the General Election of 1900. The electors of Oldham had rejected him the year before, but this time a band greeted him with 'See, the Conquering Hero Comes'. He told his audience of the hospitality shown to him by John Howard and Mr. Dewsnap of Oldham, and they roared with childlike enthusiasm that Mrs. Dewsnap was present in the hall.

The Liberals, who were campaigning against the Boer War, had little praise to spare for its heroes; some whispered that Churchill had been *forced* to resign from the army and become a newspaper correspondent; others suggested that he was too cowardly to fight the Boers as a soldier; another sneer was that his adventures were mere 'medal-snatching'—that he had got himself in and out of trouble just to collect campaign medals! But Churchill's adventurous career and his cheerful, boyish energy triumphed, and on 1st October 1900, he was elected to Parliament for the first time. The Conservatives beat the Liberals by 134 seats.

Parliament was to assemble in February, and four

months was too long for Churchill to spend in idleness. His writing had been profitable, but membership of Parliament, like a cavalry commission, was a rich man's privilege. He therefore decided to make capital out of his adventures by touring England giving lantern lectures. The halls were packed, and he could demand high fees, sometimes £300 an evening. Then he set out for America, where United States and Canadian citizens, too, flocked to hear him. When he took his seat in Parliament he had a reassuring £10,000 invested.

What spectacular novelties would this enterprising young man have to offer to Parliament?

In fact, while he was a Conservative back-bencher, Winston Churchill faithfully followed the nineteenth-century Tory policies of his father, Lord Randolph, whose speeches and writings he was now studying as preparation for the five-year task of writing his life-story. If Britain avoided ties with the other countries of Europe, argued the younger Churchill, she would keep out of wars, and therefore, being supreme at sea, would not need a large army. Another way of staying friendly with other countries was by not putting tariffs on the goods that Britain imported from those countries. In short, it was the wish of the young member for Oldham that the Government should spend as little as possible, so that there would be no need to raise income-tax, which already took away elevenpence of every pound a man earned.

Churchill made his first, or 'maiden', speech in the Commons on 18th February, three days after Parliament reassembled. The speaker before him, the fiery Liberal Lloyd George, having condemned the waste and mismanagement in South Africa and the new British trick of burning Boer farms, graciously cut short his speech out of consideration for the new member who was to follow him. Mr. Speaker therefore called Churchill's name sooner than he had expected.

Churchill rose, stammered, recovered his confidence, and delivered a well-prepared and thoroughly learned speech. He spoke as an honest soldier who had just returned from fighting a worthy enemy, and his argument was far kinder to the Boers than many of his fellow-Conservatives liked. On the subject of farm-burning, Churchill used the soldier's argument that all was fair in war. He had seen with his own eyes that the Boer War was less cruel than most. He ended with a neat reference to his father's memory.

The newspapers had already noted how much he resembled his father in style and manner. Important Liberals as well as Conservatives praised him in the speeches that followed; all of them spoke of his father, of how he had inherited his father's courage, and how, having enjoyed his illustrious father's friendship, they foresaw distinction for him too.

Afterwards Lloyd George congratulated Churchill in the smoking-room of the House. In background and upbringing the two M.P.s were as different as they could be; Lloyd George was a Welsh villager, the son of a solicitor, an ex-National-School pupil who had himself been articled to a solicitor; Churchill was an English aristocrat, the son of a lord, an ex-public schoolboy and ex-cavalry officer. But in more important ways, in character and ambitions, they were not so unlike; both were brilliant natural orators, able to hold and sway audiences at will, and both were men of burning ambition and rare courage. Lloyd George knew the common man intimately, and was bitter about the injustices he suffered; Churchill inherited his father's vision of a Merrie England in which charitable and benign nobility would some day live on friendly terms with happy and grateful working people.

An M.P. who repeatedly disagreed with members of his own party might, if he was powerful enough and popular enough with the electors, be given promotion to silence him; if he was not powerful he would merely be crushed by the strong men of his own party. Lord Randolph had gambled on his popularity, and lost.

At first, most people thought that Winston Churchill had learned the lesson. He had dedicated his *River War* to Lord Salisbury, the Conservative Prime Minister who had ruined his father. His maiden speech had steered a careful course between the Liberals who wanted peace at any price and the extreme Conservatives who thought that anyone who had a kind word for the enemy was a traitor. Young Churchill, it was felt, would be a 'safe party man'.

Only a few months after his maiden speech, however, he was delivering blistering attacks on powerful men like the Secretaries for War and for the Colonies, two of his father's bitterest enemies. The parliamentary veterans now prophesied for him the fate of his father, but he went on flaying his enemies at the rate of at least one speech a month, holding the lapels of a frock coat of the same cut as his father's, wearing his father's gold signet ring, and moving about the lobbies of the House with the same forward-leaning, impulsive walk. When Balfour, the Prime Minister, rearranged his Cabinet without nominating Churchill as a minister, many thought his fate was sealed.

Churchill's main point of disagreement with the Colonial Secretary was his determination to keep trade with foreign countries free of taxes. Chamberlain wished to 'protect' British and Empire industries by taxing foreign goods coming into Britain. For the next few months the 'Free-Traders' and the 'Protectionists' travelled the country, trying to win over the people in speech after speech.

Churchill wanted to unite all Free-Traders in the struggle, although most of the Free-Traders were Liberals. By the end of the year he had uttered the prayer, 'Thank God we have a Liberal Party!' By the following March he had made so many enemies in his own party that once, when he rose to speak, the Prime Minister and most of the Conservative members drifted away to the tea-rooms, leaving him alone with the Liberals. If there had been any doubt that he was about to become a Liberal, this deliberate insult removed it.

A month later an odd incident occurred. Churchill began a speech attacking his own party in terms far more bitter than most Liberals would have used. As members listened, recalling the cutting sarcasm of Lord Randolph in his most reckless speeches, he paused, as so often before and since, for effect. The pause was unusually prolonged. He returned to the beginning of his sentence, but got no further than before. Other members clapped to encourage him, and prompted him with suggestions. He looked at his notes, but found no help there. Finally he sat down, his speech, and even his last sentence, unfinished. The older men recalled how his father, ravaged by illness towards the end of his career, had spoken incoherently.

The true explanation was that Churchill had been in the habit of writing out his speeches in full and learning them by heart, but he had found that it was not easy for him to answer the questions and meet the challenges of those who spoke before him. Now he had begun to memorize only skeleton plans of his speeches, and to rely on the trend of the debate and on his nimble wits to supply him with the details. It was a big change of method, and it was not surprising that the first public trial was a failure.

On 31st May 1904, Churchill 'crossed the floor' of the House and became a Liberal.

At the next General Election, in January 1906, the Liberals crushed the Conservatives by 401 seats to 157. Everyone had expected a change of government, because the record of the Conservatives in the Boer War had been so bad, and because the Free-Traders had played skilfully on the people's fear that tariffs would mean dearer food, but few had expected such an overwhelming victory.

Churchill was returned by 1,241 votes as Liberal M.P. for North-West Manchester, which had returned a Conservative Member unopposed at the last election. He had published the story of his father's life the previous year, and it seems now that he ceased to be dominated by his memory. From then onwards, almost until the outbreak of the First World War, the most powerful influence on him was that of Lloyd George. The new Liberal Government was to be responsible for reforms that eased the hardships of millions of ordinary people and gave them a fairer share of the country's wealth.

CHAPTER V

Lloyd George's Partner in Office

I n the new Liberal Government Churchill became
Under-Secretary of State for the Colonies. Not only
was he now a Junior Minister, but his superior, Lord
Elgin, was in the House of Lords, which meant that
Churchill was responsible for the Colonies in the House of
Commons. His most important achievement in this office
was to give the Transvaal and the Orange Free State the
right to govern themselves. The first Prime Minister of
the Transvaal was Louis Botha, by a coincidence the very
horseman to whom Churchill had surrendered after the
armoured-train incident in South Africa.

The Conservatives wanted to delay this grant of self-
government, but Churchill triumphed. In 1910 the four
South African colonies were united, and Botha became
the first Prime Minister of the Union of South Africa.
Largely as a result of Churchill's honourable and far-
seeing treatment, South Africa was our loyal ally in both
world wars.

At that time any Bill passed by the House of Commons
had to be approved by the House of Lords. Even with the
strong Liberal Government of 1906, most of the members
of the House of Lords were Conservatives, and so they
altered or refused to pass many new measures that the

Liberals had passed in the Commons. The Liberal Prime Minister, Sir Henry Campbell-Bannerman, tried to lessen the power of the Lords, and Churchill, the son of a lord, supported him with a brilliant, slashing speech. Bannerman died, however, in 1908, leaving the Lords as powerful as ever.

On the death of the Prime Minister, Lloyd George became Chancellor of the Exchequer and Churchill succeeded him in the Cabinet post of President of the Board of Trade. Nowadays when an M.P. becomes a Cabinet Minister he holds his seat in Parliament without a new election, but in 1908 the rules obliged Churchill to fight a by-election. With his fame and skill as a speaker, he was expected to win comfortably at North-West Manchester.

Unfortunately for him, the 'suffragettes' made him one of their favourite victims. No woman at that time was allowed to vote at elections, but there was a number of intelligent and determined women who were furious at this injustice. From the 1906 election onwards they sought by every means in their power to win the right to vote for their sex. They tried to burst into the Houses of Parliament, attacked policemen who tried to stop them, chained themselves to railings in public places and poured acid into letter-boxes. One woman threw herself in front of the King's horse at the Derby, and was killed.

The leaders of the movement, Mrs. Pankhurst and her two daughters, were members of a well-known Manchester family, and besides, the suffragettes were more Conservative than Liberal. So they gave the man who had crossed the floor of the House special attention. They interrupted his speeches to shout for votes for women. In vain Churchill declared himself on their side; they wanted him to promise them the vote, which, of course, it was not in his power to give. The outcome was that he lost the Manchester seat.

The same evening a telegram came from Scottish Liberals in Dundee inviting him to stand for them. This time Churchill's votes numbered almost as many as those of the Conservative and Socialist candidates added together. Even here the suffragettes pestered him, and a pretty Irish girl named Malony accompanied his speeches with a clanging dinner bell.

While campaigning in Dundee Churchill met Miss Clementine Hozier, the granddaughter of the Countess of Airlie. They fell in love at first sight, and were married at St. Margaret's, Westminster. At the end of his book *My Early Life*, Churchill recalls 'September, 1908, when I married and lived happily ever afterwards'. Behind the turbulent career of a dynamic man of genius there is often a calm, utterly devoted wife and companion such as Lady Churchill, claiming no credit for his eminence, yet indispensable to it.

When Lloyd George became Chancellor of the Exchequer in Asquith's government and Churchill succeeded him as President of the Board of Trade, the natural attraction these two fiery, hard-hitting speakers had for each other grew into a close partnership. At the Board of Trade Lloyd George had striven to improve conditions for working people, especially merchant seamen and dockers. Churchill took over and completed many of his projects.

Even in 1909 there were rules, known as Factory Acts, which limited hours of work and ensured that there was reasonable comfort in the factories; but these rules did not protect those workers, mainly women, who worked cruelly long hours for absurdly low wages in the slums of the great cities. There had been talk of setting up committees called Trade Boards to look after them, but nothing had been done. It was the responsibility of the Home Office, but Churchill did not see why, as President of *the* Board of Trade, he should not busy himself with Trade Boards, and in his dynamic way he hustled a Trade Boards Act through Parliament for which thousands have been grateful.

Two Socialist thinkers, Beatrice and Sidney Webb, had declared that there should be offices which employers could notify of the kinds and numbers of workers they needed, and to which workers who had left one job could go to find another. Once again a man of energy and drive was needed to put a fine and original idea into action, and once again Churchill supplied the need. Not many people nowadays realize that the Labour Exchanges owed much to Winston Churchill, the lifelong anti-Socialist.

Before these stirring Edwardian times, if a working man lost his job and could not find another, he had to live on his savings or sell his belongings, and when his money was spent, he had to go to the workhouse with his family. Churchill now planned for a system of unemployment insurance, while Lloyd George set about providing funds for workers and their families to live on when they were out of work through illness.

The mainly Conservative House of Lords disliked these important changes, and blocked every Bill that was sent up to them by the Commons. In 1908 Churchill spent some time at the home of Lloyd George in South Wales. It was probably there and then that their campaign against the power of the Lords was planned. In attacking the Conservatives, Lloyd George and Churchill had to be very careful, because the Liberals had lost a great deal of popularity since the election. Lloyd George had been labelled a Socialist, and a Socialist at that time was a sort of 'bogeyman', even for working people, while nannies in well-to-do families threatened the children with, 'If you aren't good, Lloyd George will get you!' Besides, the newspapers were full of the new threat to peace from Germany; it was known that very few Liberals liked spending money on preparing for war, and that some of them were outright pacifists who would have nothing to do with war. Many people were afraid that the Liberals would let the Germans overrun the country. Then all their plans for making life easier for ordinary people would come to nothing.

In 1909 Lloyd George, as Chancellor of the Exchequer, put his budget before the Commons. It penalized the rich by increasing tax on high incomes and by making luxuries dearer. Death duties, the money paid on fortunes left in wills, were increased. All this was enough to anger the Lords, but the last straw was the Land Tax, which now had to be paid by the owners of undeveloped land and by those whose land became more valuable year by year. When the great landowners, the dukes, protested, Lloyd George lashed them savagely in speech after speech; but when Churchill joined in the merciless attacks on the dukes, his opponents were able to point out that he himself was a member of a ducal family, and to condemn him as a traitor to his class. He and Mrs. Churchill were shunned by the aristocracy into which they had been born.

Churchill has never been daunted by unpopularity, however, and the two reformers pressed on with their campaign. It was largely due to their brilliance that the Liberal Government was able, by clever manœuvring, to compel the House of Lords to pass a Bill which lessened their own power; in future they could not block any Bill after the Commons had passed it three times, or any Bill dealing with financial matters if the Commons had passed it once.

Churchill was promoted from the Board of Trade to the Home Office at the January election. There he was responsible for the Mines Accidents Act, which tightened the safety, rescue and first-aid regulations in the coal mines. The danger of explosions, and the more gradual but no less terrible effects of coal dust on miners' lungs, were lessened by the Coal Mines Act in the following year. Boys under fourteen could no longer be employed in the mines.

During these years there was rioting and bitterness in the South Wales mines which threatened to become revolution. Now Churchill is by nature and training a military officer, accustomed to command rather than persuade. He likes quick decisions and the most direct routes to success. He sent five hundred Metropolitan Police and two squadrons of Hussars to reinforce the police on the spot, and, very wisely, a senior army officer, General Sir Nevil Macready, to command this force, with instructions not to use the cavalry if the police could handle the situation. In fact, the police were so heavily stoned that Macready had to use his troops. The soldiers used their bayonets, but in such a way that no casualties were reported, though some of the rioters could not sit down comfortably for some days.

Still, it was an undeniable fact that troops had been used, and that those troops had used the bayonet. The Home Secretary and former President of the Board of Trade who had worked so hard with Lloyd George to make life happier for the working people was now represented as their enemy. The Conservatives, too, criticized him for not having used troops earlier and more decisively to stamp out the rioting!

48

Less serious, though no less Churchillian, was the quaint interlude known as 'The Siege of Sidney Street'. At ten o'clock on the morning of 3rd January 1911, violent knocking on his front door disturbed Churchill in his bath. Dripping, and with only a towel round him, the Home Secretary heard what was, in peaceful pre-1914 London, an amazing story.

A gang of desperate foreign criminals led by a Russian nicknamed 'Peter the Painter' had tried to break into a jeweller's shop in Houndsditch, in the East End. Three of the policemen who tried to arrest them had been shot and killed. Then the burglars had barricaded themselves in a house in Sidney Street, a street linking Mile End Road and Commercial Road, with plenty of arms, ammunition and home-made bombs, and had been holding off the police with gunfire since three in the morning. They had already killed another policeman when Churchill was informed.

The Home Secretary at once gave permission for troops to be used, and a detachment of Scots Guards was hurried from the Tower of London. Twenty minutes after leaving his bath Churchill was at the Home Office, setting up a battle headquarters. The situation was not clear, so, in astrakhan-collared coat and top hat, he set out to see for himself.

He found police with shotguns commandeered from a gunsmith's shop and guardsmen with rifles firing steadily into 100 Sidney Street, and the answering shots whining off the dingy buildings. Soon he was among them, peering up the street from doubtful cover. A brewery opposite the house was occupied, and the bullets were pumped in from there.

Churchill, who afterwards admitted that strong curiosity as well as a sense of duty had brought him on the

D   49

scene, now found himself in an awkward predicament; the officers in charge of the troops and the police were the proper persons to give orders, and yet he, as the Home Secretary, was their superior. Characteristically, he assumed command, and ordered that metal sheets from a nearby foundry should be used as shields for an advance on the besieged house. For good measure he called for field guns and Royal Engineers, but before the operation could be conducted on this scale, smoke was seen to be coming from a window of Number 100.

Firemen were soon on the scene, eager to do their duty, but to avoid further loss of life Churchill decided that the house was to be allowed to burn. After a time firing from the house ceased, and a police inspector, followed by the Home Secretary and a police sergeant with a shotgun, entered the burning building. They found the charred corpses of two of the gangsters. One had been shot, the other suffocated. Peter the Painter himself had escaped.

Balfour, the leader of the Conservatives, was sarcastic in Parliament about Churchill's role in the incident; he had seen photographs in the papers, he remarked, and while the photographer's presence there was understandable, the Home Secretary's was not. Balfour and other critics were right; the incident was the concern of less important officials than the principal Secretary of State. But Churchill without his appetite for excitement and danger would be a lesser man.

The Conservatives had taunted Churchill for his slowness in ordering troops into action in South Wales. Perhaps he remembered this in August 1911, when dockers and railwaymen were on strike; for, without being asked by the local authorities, he sent troops to all points where they were needed to keep the trains running. Again there was a storm of criticism.

When he explained this hasty action to Parliament, it became clear that he had seen himself as the commander-in-chief of a military operation. Ramsay Macdonald, the Labour leader, bitterly attacked him, reminding him that England was not Russia or Germany, and accusing him of not knowing what civil liberty meant. Lloyd George was called to the rescue, and, with his deeper understanding of the feelings of the people, averted a general strike.

There is no doubt that Churchill's period as Home Secretary was the least successful of his public life so far. He came to the office at a time when the pattern of English society was changing more rapidly than it had ever done, when ordinary people were claiming a share in the government of the country and becoming less willing blindly to obey orders from those in power. His restless energy, his urge to get things done in the most direct way, had done wonders to improve the lot of the people, yet when he left the Home Office for the Admiralty in October 1911, he was much less popular than he had been before.

CHAPTER VI

At the Admiralty in Peacetime

To understand Churchill's appointment as First Lord of the Admiralty, one must glance at the course of foreign affairs during the ten years since he entered political life.

Throughout history France had been Britain's closest and most powerful enemy, but in 1904 the two countries had concluded a series of agreements called the *Entente Cordiale*, or 'friendly understanding', mainly to safeguard each other's possessions in North Africa and to keep Germany out. Germany was alarmed at the way the French were gaining influence in Morocco, and in 1906 a perilous arrangement was made whereby France and Germany shared control of that country.

Two years later the Sultan of Morocco was overthrown by his brother, who, finding that he could not govern unaided, asked France for help. Germany watched suspiciously as French troops were shipped to Morocco, and announced that she had sent a gunboat, the *Panther*, to the Moroccan port of Agadir. The danger of war seemed very real.

The British Army was ready, for Haldane, Secretary of State for War for the past five years, had thoroughly reformed it and, working with French staff officers, had made a plan to put a British expeditionary force on the left wing of the French Army if war should break out. Railway arrangements had been worked out to the minute for moving the British troops in France, with time even allowed for coffee halts.

Unfortunately this was purely an army plan. The army and navy had so little to do with each other that no arrangements had been made to ship the expeditionary force to France! Admiral Lord Fisher, the old sea-dog who had been First Sea Lord until his retirement in 1910, and whose ideas and formidable personality still ruled the navy, had always been against sending troops to France.

Haldane threatened the Prime Minister that unless the navy established a war staff such as existed for the army, he would resign. He put his own name forward as the best man for the post of First Lord of the Admiralty, but the cautious Prime Minister was afraid that to send the army chief to lick the navy into shape would be a terrible insult to the admirals. Failing Haldane, the need was for some other man with the energy and drive to get his own way with the difficult, stubborn disciples of Fisher. The outcome was that Churchill became First Lord of the Admiralty in October 1911, at the age of thirty-six.

It is amusing to reflect that the Germans were not displeased by this appointment. As a Conservative M.P. he had tried to carry on his father's policies, one of which had been to use the army as a police force in the colonies and keep out of trouble in Europe. As a Liberal Minister Winston Churchill had helped Lloyd George to spend money on popular social reforms rather than on armaments. Twice, in 1906 and 1908, he had been the Kaiser's personal guest in Germany, and had watched troop manœuvres at the Kaiser's side.

Almost immediately after his appointment as First

Lord, Churchill invited Fisher out of retirement to act as his unofficial adviser. Fisher and Churchill had a great deal in common, despite a difference in age of forty-four years; both were men of phenomenal energy and stubborn determination; both could be rude and arrogant; and both were open to new ideas, especially technical novelties in warfare. Naval officers whom Fisher liked were said to be 'in the Fishpond'; not only was he unashamed of favouritism, but he even claimed that it was the secret of efficiency!

It is not surprising, then, that the association of these two extraordinary men was one of warm friendship or heated quarrelling; there was no middle way.

Fisher's two pet ambitions were the introduction of fifteen-inch guns and the conversion of naval units from coal to oil fuel. With Churchill as the navy's spokesman in Parliament, both were quickly realized. Opponents pointed out that we had our own supplies of coal, and that a war might cut us off from oil. Churchill immediately sent experts to Persia. They reported that the Persian oilfields could be developed at a cost of 2 million pounds. When Parliament debated the project in June 1914, many voices were raised against such extravagance, but Churchill had his way, and Britain has never regretted her bargain.

At such times the Admiralty was a harmonious place; when Churchill interfered in naval appointments it was not. Once Fisher discovered that his Minister had given important positions to three officers who were not in the Fishpond. In a fury he threw up his unofficial post and went back into retirement in Naples. Churchill, who was cruising with Asquith, the Prime Minister, in the Admiralty yacht *Enchantress*, called there to reason with him. It was useless. Asquith himself tried. The result was the same. What higher authority than the Prime Minister could prevail on the stubborn old man?

On Sunday, in the English church of Naples, the preacher's eye sought Fisher out among the congregation, and his stern voice thundered that no man in his full vigour had the right to forsake his duty to his country and his countrymen. Fisher, a simple man beneath the ferocity, yielded and returned to his work at the Admiralty. The preacher's sentences may have been pure coincidence, but it is hard to believe that Churchill had not had a private word with him before the service.

The Government was held to ransom by the Irish Nationalist movement while it was making these strenuous efforts towards national security. The Liberals had won only two seats more than the Conservatives in the election of 1910, and so they had to rely for their power to govern on the forty-two Labour members and the eighty-four Irish Nationalists. The Irishmen demanded Home Rule for their country as the price of their support for the Parliament Act limiting the power of the House of Lords and for the National Insurance Act.

To win back the popularity his heavy spending on the navy had lost him in the Liberal party, and attracted, as always, by the prospect of a stirring fight, Churchill threw himself heartily into the struggle for Home Rule.

The northern province of Ulster, which was Protestant, and friendly with England, did not want Home Rule, as it would mean joining the Catholics of the south. Never lacking in courage, Churchill tried to make a speech in the Ulster Hall in Belfast, the capital of Ulster, but the angry northerners threatened to break up the meeting, and he had to address his audience in a hired marquee. In one Commons debate at this time an Ulster M.P. hit Churchill on the head with a well-aimed book, and the infuriated

First Lord was only prevented from striking back by his own supporters. The book was a manual of rules for the observance of good order in parliamentary debates!

By late 1913 a force of 100,000 men, called the Ulster Volunteers, was being armed by Germany, who wanted England to have a civil war on her hands. The Volunteers seized ports on the Irish north-east coast in April 1914, while in Dublin the southern Irish were flocking to enlist in the Irish Nationalist Army. Civil war seemed certain. Events were taking place elsewhere, however, which made the Irish troubles seem much less important.

We usually think of the 1914–18 war as a struggle fought out mainly in France and Flanders between Britain, France and their allies on the one hand and Germany and her allies on the other. It is mystifying to learn that the war was started by the assassination of the Archduke Franz Ferdinand of Austria and his wife by a Bosnian Serb in the capital of Bosnia, in the south-eastern corner of a Europe that has since changed many of its names and frontiers; but the connection of this incident with the German attack on France can be traced.

Since the late nineteenth century, Germany's population and industries had been growing faster than those of any other European country. The German Emperor believed that his country's trade and influence should expand towards the Near and Middle East, and he was determined that Germany should have her way, by friendship or by force, with the countries that lay on the broad south-eastern path out of Europe. Friendship was already established with Austria-Hungary, the sprawling empire immediately south-east of Germany, and with Turkey, the Near-Eastern country with a foothold in Europe. Unfortunately for the Kaiser's plans, between Austria-Hungary and Turkey stretched a barrier of smaller states, from Albania, on the Adriatic Sea, to Rumania, bordering on Russia. Russia relied on this barrier to hold Germany and Austria-Hungary back. Serbia, the leader of the barrier states, had not forgiven Austria-Hungary for having taken possession of Bosnia, with its largely-Serb population, in 1908.

On 28th June 1914, the Archduke Franz Ferdinand, nephew and heir of the Austrian emperor, and his wife were shot while visiting Sarajevo, capital of Bosnia. The assassin, who belonged to a group of nationalists controlled by a Serbian secret society called the 'Black Hand', had just returned from Belgrade, capital of Serbia, with an accomplice. Members of the Serbian Government seem to have known of the plot before the two youths left Serbia, but had failed to have them arrested, and had sent no proper warning to Sarajevo.

After the crime Germany encouraged Austria to crush Serbia. Austria threatened Serbia with war if she did not agree to a number of demands, which included the right to send investigators into Serbia. The Serbian Government sent a soft answer to turn away Austrian wrath, but refused to allow the investigation. Germany, surprisingly, told Austria that there was now no excuse for starting a war, but the Austrians ignored them and declared war on Serbia.

The powder train that was to lead to the explosion in western Europe was now ignited. Russia had massed troops on her frontier with Germany as well as her frontier with Austria. Germany ordered her to disperse them, and declared war when she refused. France was bound by a twenty-year-old treaty to help Russia, but before she could act, German cavalry crossed the French frontier at three points on 1st–2nd August. This move was a feint, for the main German thrust was to take the easy way into France, across neutral Belgium. Belgium was invaded on the morning of 4th August.

Why did the powerful, aggressive Germany try to prevent Austria from starting war, after urging her to seize the excuse to crush Serbia? At least partly because, while the British Liberal Cabinet was looking for ways of avoiding war, Churchill in mid-July had ordered a mobilization exercise for the Main Fleet and the Second and Third Reserve Fleets. On 20th July, after the review by the King at Spithead, Churchill ordered the ships of the Fleet not to disperse but to stay near their home ports. When Austria attacked Serbia, the Fleet secretly left Portland, again on the orders of the First Lord and without the backing of the Cabinet, and sailed through the Channel and up to the Scapa Flow, safe from any German trap.

The Cabinet as a whole did not agree that Britain would have to fight. A group of pacifist ministers wanted the country to stay out of the war. Another group had simply not made up its mind. Only Churchill was resigned to the worst. On 1st August he warned the Admiralty to be ready to mobilize the reserves, expecting the orders to be given by the Cabinet that morning; but he was wrong. On 2nd August the Cabinet learned that Germany had declared war on Russia. Churchill went to Downing Street and told the Prime Minister that he was going to complete mobilization immediately, without Cabinet consent. The Cabinet gave its consent to this action the following day—after he had acted!

On 3rd August Sir Edward Grey, the Foreign Secretary, told the House of Commons that Britain would stand by France if Germany attacked her. The next morning Grey asked Germany to say by eleven o'clock the same night whether she would keep out of Belgium, but by two in the afternoon he knew that Germans were on Belgian soil. The Prime Minister and Grey waited in the Cabinet Room at Number Ten, Churchill elsewhere in Whitehall. Big Ben boomed eleven. No reply had come from Germany, and therefore Britain was at war.

CHAPTER VII

At the Admiralty
in the First World War

I n the midst of calamity the First Lord could feel satisfied that he had done his duty. The mighty British Fleet, ready in advance, kept the German Navy penned in its own harbours. Only those German vessels that were already on the high seas were able to give any trouble, and that only for a short time; in fact, Jutland was the only naval battle the Germans risked with the British throughout the war. The British admirals, and most of the British public, believed that it was the navy's task to police the seas in this way, and not to go looking for trouble. Churchill, however, spoiling for a fight, sent his cruisers into the waters of the Heligoland Bight, where they sank three German cruisers and put three more out of action.

The British Expeditionary Force, which, if there had been war before Churchill came to the Admiralty, would have had no means of crossing the Channel, was put into France without a single loss, and joined the French left flank at Mons, just over the Belgian border.

It was this left flank that bore the brunt of Germany's surprise thrust through Belgium. Under heavy attack the French broke contact with the British, who escaped encirclement and capture only by a brilliant but costly withdrawal from Mons. After this, the German right was able to cross the frontier into France. Meanwhile their centre had crossed Luxemburg and the difficult Ardennes country, but their left made less headway in the mountainous and heavily fortified country close to France's frontier with Germany, where France had been prepared for attack.

The result was that the German front swung round until it was facing south. Intending at this time to smash the French armies and take Paris, they found their advance checked by the River Aisne. South of the Aisne, and roughly parallel to it, was the River Marne, a desperate last line of defence for the French, for it ran from the mountains of the frontier country almost to the suburbs of Paris. In the last days of August the Allied defence of the Aisne crumbled, and the Germans poured southwards to the River Marne. The French Government left Paris for Bordeaux in the south-west.

From 6th September to 12th September the French and British defended the vital line of the Marne and flung the invaders back to the Aisne. The battle of the Aisne ended in deadlock, and trench warfare began; this part of the Western Front was to remain almost stationary, within a few miles of the Aisne, for the remaining four years of the war. Each side now began to move out to its left to try to get behind its enemy's right flank, and each move was swiftly countered, so that the battlefront was lengthened at each end until it met an obstacle. The Swiss frontier was quickly reached at the south-eastern end; in the northwest the race for the Channel was on, each side hurrying to anchor its coastal flank as far forward as it could.

While the Western Front was taking shape in September, news of the 'Dunkirk Circus' became public. The German sweep into France had left the French port of Dunkirk high and dry, so that any force in Dunkirk could harass the German lines of communication from the flank. The French commander-in-chief asked for a British force to be landed there, and as army troops could not be spared, Kitchener asked Churchill for marines.

Any positive action was welcome to the First Lord. He sent not only a brigade of marines, but fifty London buses to move them about rapidly, enabling them to pop up at many different towns on the northern part of the Franco-Belgian frontier. The Germans were convinced that their right flank was threatened by 40,000 troops! Churchill visited his 'Dunkirk Circus' as often as he could in person.

With London buses in action on the Continent, Churchill's critics felt that the limit of eccentricity had been reached. They were wrong.

The Germans laid siege to Antwerp on 28th September as part of their plan to seize the Channel ports, and the Belgians sent a despairing appeal to the British and French, saying that they would have to surrender unless help arrived immediately. Churchill was *en route* for Dover and Dunkirk on 2nd October when his special train was ordered back to London. Kitchener wanted him to go to Antwerp at midnight and, with the help of a brigade of marines, persuade the Belgians not to yield. At the same time the British commander-in-chief in France was ordered to send forces through Lille to Antwerp, though these would not arrive for three or four days.

At one o'clock the next afternoon a large open car, horn blaring madly, hurtled through the Antwerp streets, taking corners on two wheels. A sandy-haired man leaped out before it came to a halt and charged into the Belgian headquarters with arms outstretched. Churchill had arrived to take over the Belgian defence.

Without delay he sent a message to the Prime Minister asking to be relieved of his post at the Admiralty and given command of the Allied relief force on its way to Antwerp. Everyone in the city was acting on his orders—not only the soldiers and sailors, but the Belgian king and his ministers! But Asquith refused to give the ex-lieutenant of cavalry command over two major-generals and other senior officers, although Kitchener was willing to promote him to the rank of major-general for the task.

Churchill now wired to Kitchener for two naval brigades. These troops, mainly inexperienced, fought gallantly, and though the Germans captured the city after five days and went on to take Zeebrugge and Ostend, they could not overcome the defences of Nieuport, the last Belgian coastal town before the French frontier, where the Belgians kept them back by damming the river Yser at its mouth and causing it to flood its banks for the last ten miles of its course. Twenty miles inland, the first battle of Ypres, which raged through late October and early November, finally established the northern end of the Allied line at Nieuport, and the four-year stalemate on the Western Front had begun.

Losses in Antwerp had been so heavy that it was easy for Churchill's enemies to represent him as a danger to his country; yet his five days there almost certainly saved many more casualties later. It was easy, too, for critics to claim at this time that while his mind was full of spectacular adventures on land, he was neglecting his proper duty, the conduct of the war at sea.

The *Emden* and the *Königsberg* were wreaking havoc in the Indian Ocean, the *Scharnhorst* and the *Gneisenau* were preying on shipping off West Africa, and the *Goeben* and the *Breslau* had sneaked through the Dardanelles into the

Sea of Marmora. It was whispered that the First Sea Lord, Prince Louis of Battenberg, was not strong enough to hold his own with Churchill. Though this argument was probably only a cloak for the feeling that a man of German origin should not have a key post in the conduct of the war, Prince Louis resigned, and in November Churchill invited Fisher to take his place.

From then until the end of their association either Churchill or Fisher was on duty at the Admiralty at all times of the day or night, with an agreement that all decisions should be approved by both men. Fisher, dynamic as ever, hustled on the building of new ships. At the back of his mind was a war-winning plan—a combined operation to land troops on Germany's Baltic shore within a hundred miles of Berlin. Such a bold idea could not fail to capture the imagination of Churchill, who was just as enthusiastic about it as Fisher. The Admiralty was a happy as well as a busy place again.

The Baltic plan was fraught with risks; if it had ever been put into action it could hardly have been more disastrous than the one that replaced it.

On 31st October Turkey had entered the war as an ally of Germany, and a month later the name 'Dardanelles' was heard in the War Council. The Dardanelles are the straits which lead from the Aegean Sea to the Sea of Marmora. At the other end of the Sea of Marmora are the shorter, narrower straits of the Bosphorus, which lead past the Turkish capital, Constantinople, to the Black Sea. All the shores of these straits and the Sea of Marmora were Turkish. It occurred to Churchill that if the Allies could blast their way through the Dardanelles and capture Constantinople, they might be joined by Bulgaria, Greece, Rumania and Italy.

Fisher clung to his Baltic project. Lloyd George

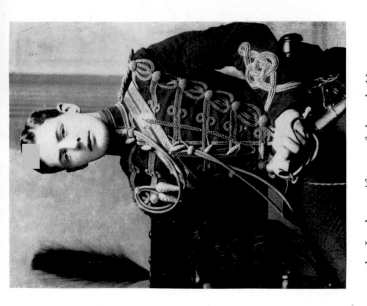

1a. As a schoolboy

1b. In the uniform of the 4th Hussars

2a. With other British and French officers during the First
World War

2b. With Lloyd George in Whitehall, October, 1915

favoured a thrust through the Balkans. Kitchener put a damper on all three schemes by refusing to divert any troops from the Western Front.

In January our ally Russia, hard pressed by the Turks in the Caucasus, asked for help. When the British and French had been in desperate straits at Mons, Russia had made Germany look over her shoulder by attacking East Prussia; therefore we were bound in honour to come to her aid.

Stout old Fisher put aside his Baltic plan and produced a scheme for combined operations against Turkey necessitating the forcing of the Dardanelles with a fleet of out-of-date battleships, the use of 75,000 of our own troops, and the support of Greece and Bulgaria. The scheme had glaring weaknesses; the Russians did not want the Greeks as allies, Bulgaria was more likely to side with the Germans, and Kitchener was still unwilling to release troops from France.

Churchill was attracted by the naval role in this plan. He wired Admiral Carden, in command at the Dardanelles, to find out whether the old ships could batter a way through without the army. Carden replied that a once-for-all dash would fail, but that if the defences were destroyed stage by stage they might succeed.

At a fateful meeting of the War Council on 13th January it was decided that a naval expedition should take the Gallipoli peninsula. It was never made clear how the navy was to 'take' a tongue of land about fifty miles long and at one point about fifteen miles wide. The taking of Gallipoli and the forcing of the Dardanelles were really two separate tasks.

Churchill saw the whole operation through rose-tinted spectacles. *If* the navy got through the Dardanelles, the Greeks *might* join us. *If* the navy threatened Constantinople, there *might* be a Turkish revolt. *If* all this happened, the army would not be needed.

In February, Fisher, overjoyed by an announcement from Kitchener that troops could at last be spared from France, urged Churchill to agree to combined operations, but the First Lord was now firmly wedded to his naval plan.

On 19th February the navy opened its bombardment of the outer fortresses of the Dardanelles. On the 24th Kitchener promised that the army would 'see the business through' if the navy failed. By the beginning of March the outer fortresses were knocked out, but the remaining defences proved much tougher.

Carden was taken ill, and his second-in-command, Admiral de Robeck, took charge. He launched an all-day attack on 18th March with the whole Allied fleet, and by late afternoon had almost silenced the shore guns. The ships moved forward confidently. Suddenly they found themselves in a minefield. Three battleships went to the bottom, and three others were crippled. De Robeck informed the Admiralty that floating mines necessitated a change of plan. He would have to delay the advance for a few days.

Four days later, however, when General Sir Ian Hamilton, who had arrived at the Dardanelles to report on the possibility of the Army's taking part, consulted with de Robeck, they decided that the naval onslaught should be postponed until the army could join in. Churchill, on receiving this frustrating message, wanted to wire de Robeck to continue, but Fisher and other admirals would not overrule the admiral on the spot, and the telegram was not sent.

For five weeks nothing was done. Then the expeditionary force arrived, with only the haziest instructions from the War Office, much of it based on inaccurate maps. Indeed, the first trustworthy maps the British used were taken from Turkish prisoners! Transport and equipment was not sent in the same boats as the troops it was intended for, and arrived days later. Much of it was in any case quite unsuitable for the rocky heights of Gallipoli. Meanwhile the Turks, grateful for the advance warning of the troop landings, were strengthening their defences.

Hamilton successfully landed 29,000 men on the Gallipoli beaches on 25th April, but the casualties were heavy, and little advance could be made. In the following month Fisher protested about the drain of ships and men for the Dardanelles, declaring that he had been against the campaign from the beginning. Churchill pointed out that his First Sea Lord had agreed in writing to every move.

The same night Churchill took certain decisions about movements of ships without consulting Fisher, who was resting. As soon as Fisher heard of this the next morning, he resigned, shut himself in his official residence and refused to see anyone. After pleading with him in vain by letter, Churchill chose a new Admiralty Board and a new First Sea Lord.

The Conservatives, who liked Fisher as warmly as they hated Churchill, now said that they would no longer support the Government if Fisher went and Churchill stayed; and when Churchill went to the House of Commons to announce his new Admiralty Board, the Prime Minister told him that the political parties were to join forces in a Coalition Government, and that he would not be First Lord in that government. Lloyd George tried to persuade Asquith to give him an important Ministry, but the Conservatives were out for blood, and the Prime Minister weakly yielded to them by offering him the

Chancellorship of the Duchy of Lancaster, a post with few duties and few powers.

As a member of the War Council, however, Churchill could still urge that the Gallipoli operations should continue. There matters were going from bad to worse. The army and the navy were reinforced repeatedly, but too late each time; Churchill wrote later that each week's delay increased the need by one division. The troops were finally evacuated in December, having achieved nothing and having suffered a quarter of a million casualties.

When each side revealed its secrets to the other after the war, the enemy version of the Dardanelles exploit made bitter reading for Churchill and other members of the War Council. On the evening of 18th March, after the Allied ships had battered the Dardanelles defences mercilessly throughout the day, the Turks were completely demoralized, half their ammunition was used up and the control of their guns was in chaos. Even the Germans were sure that the next day's naval onslaught was bound to succeed. The minefield had been sown six months earlier, and many of the mines had been carried away or had sunk too deep to be dangerous, so that the sinking and crippling of the six ships had been extraordinarily bad luck. No one had been more astonished than the defenders of the fortresses when the attack was not resumed.

On the other hand, the German general who commanded the Dardanelles defence wrote afterwards that the naval action at the Dardanelles could only have been effective if troops had been landed beforehand or at the same time. Troops were beginning to be available from the Western Front when the naval assault began, and if Churchill had been less impatient and less determined on a purely naval operation, such landings could have been made.

After evacuation was decided upon, Churchill was no longer a member of the War Committee which replaced the ill-fated War Council. Restless and discontented in his office of Chancellor of the Duchy of Lancaster, he resigned, made a farewell speech in Parliament, and prepared for active service on the Western Front.

Three days later the Churchill household was in confusion as Major Churchill of the Oxfordshire Yeomanry packed for France. His secretary was in tears. Lady Randolph was distraught at her son's fall from the highest places to that of a soldier in the trenches. Only Mrs. Churchill carried out her tasks with unshakable calm.

CHAPTER VIII

Deadlock, and the Solution: Trench Warfare and Tanks

As soon as Churchill arrived in France he was taken to meet the Commander-in-Chief, General Sir John French, who offered him the command of an infantry brigade. This was a considerable command for an officer who had left the army as a lieutenant, and Churchill asked if he might spend a month in the trenches first, attached to a Guards battalion.

Guards officers are a proud and exclusive body of men with jealously preserved traditions. Churchill had the breeding and background of a gentleman, it was true, and he had been a cavalry subaltern; but since then he had been a politician, and, even worse, he had forsaken the Conservatives for the Liberals.

He joined his Grenadier battalion as they moved towards the battle-front in a chilly November drizzle, and rode with the commanding officer behind the troops. After half an hour's stony silence his companion said curtly, 'I think I ought to tell you we were not at all consulted in the matter of your coming to join us.'

Churchill did not mind this icy welcome; indeed, he was amused during the next few days by his fellow-officers' efforts to show him that only his rank and his behaviour mattered to them, ex-Cabinet Minister or not. The truth was that the whole battalion, officers and men, were intensely interested in this creature from another world.

Even above battalion level, curiosity sometimes got the better of politeness. The general commanding the corps once summoned him to a crossroads where a car was to pick him up and take him to a meeting-place. After plodding three miles through mud, exposed to fire, and after an hour's wait at the crossroads, Churchill was told by a staff officer that the car had been sent to the wrong place, and that the interview was cancelled. There was no pressing reason for the interview. The general simply wanted to meet an ex-Minister! Furious at this treatment, Churchill trudged back—to be greeted with congratulations and the news that a shell had crashed into his dugout just after he left.

His cheerfulness and unassuming manner very soon persuaded his fellow-officers to accept him as one of their number. When the second-in-command of the battalion went on leave, the commanding officer asked Churchill to take over his duties, and reported at the end of his 'probation' period that he was well fitted to command a brigade. Questions were asked in Parliament, however, about this lightning promotion; Asquith, as so often before, yielded to the Conservative outcry and persuaded Sir John French to offer Churchill only a battalion.

The Royal Scots Fusiliers did not welcome him much more warmly than the Grenadiers had done; but this time the thaw came much more quickly. The day after his arrival he assembled his officers in the ramshackle farmhouse which was the battalion headquarters, and delivered a brilliant lecture on—lice! After hearing the life-story of the louse and the important role it had played in

71

the history of warfare, his audience accepted him without reserve, and were completely won over later by his 'off-parade' charm and kindliness at dinner in H.Q. Mess. The men were overawed at first by the presence of such an eminent man, but they too were soon put at their ease by the Colonel's way of getting to know individual men by asking them friendly questions.

In the trenches of Ploegsteert, or 'Plug Street', as the British found it easier to call it, Churchill smartened the battalion up by driving officers and men hard. Orders for new forms of defence and new ways of sandbag-building poured from battalion headquarters, some of them unsuccessful, others life-savers. The new commanding officer drove himself at least as hard as he did others, and seemed unaware of danger. In a suit of waterproof overalls and a light-blue French shrapnel helmet, the forerunners of a succession of bizarre clothes and headgear which were to become part of the Churchill legend, he did the rounds of his battalion three times a day, and nothing that was going on escaped him.

At his 'rest' headquarters in the buildings of a convent a thousand yards from the enemy lines, Churchill was writing a paper one day on the use of the tank when a shell burst less than fifty yards away. He could have taken shelter in the cellar below, but preferred to go to the battalion office in another building. When he got back to his room he found that a thirty-pound shell had crashed through it and into the cellar, where it lay unexploded.

Ever since his schooldays Churchill had felt certain that he was destined for greatness; and, logically, each time he escaped death by some stroke of chance, his conviction grew that he was being 'spared' for some glorious future task. One night, when the sky was filled with coloured rockets, 'whizzbangs' and other projectiles, he suggested to his adjutant that they stand on the fire-step and watch. While the adjutant, as he confessed later, was horrified by the projectiles flying around them, Churchill enjoyed every perilous moment, and inquired in a casual tone whether his companion liked war!

Generals and other high-ranking officers commonly dined at this unusual battalion commander's headquarters, and it was his habit to offer them an after-dinner entertainment they could hardly refuse, whatever their private feelings; he led them on a tour of his battalion area—a crawl across mud and through barbed wire that plucked at their uniforms, with Very lights playing on the red and gold that denoted their seniority.

Other visitors, politicians from home, persuaded Churchill that he was wasting his talents as an obscure battalion commander; and when, in the summer of 1916, his unit was amalgamated with another and he found himself without a command, he asked the War Minister for his discharge. If the minister had refused this very irregular request, he might have been accused of keeping a formidable member of the Opposition out of Parliament for his own ends. In June 1916, Churchill was back in England as a civilian.

During the next month a bloody and fruitless battle began on the Somme in northern France which was to last five months and cost the lives of half a million British troops, thrown hopelessly against strongly fortified German positions. Churchill's campaign against this stupidity only aroused resentment against himself.

While he was First Lord, Churchill had turned his active imagination to the problem of the stalemate in the trenches. A suggestion of his that two steam-rollers should be bolted together side by side and used for demolishing the enemy's trenches had reached the trial stage, but the monster had stuck in the mud. When he gave orders for the building of armoured cars with portable bridging material, the Admiralty found enough fault with the idea to turn it down. An army officer's mention of the idea of 'land battleships' in a conversation with Churchill had brought into being the 'Admiralty Landships Committee', through which eighteen 'landships' of two types, one wheeled and the other tracked, were ordered. His successor at the Admiralty reduced the order to a single machine, and the 'landships' became known as 'Winston's folly'.

In February, however, when Churchill was still on active service, King George V had seen this solitary 'landship', the caterpillar-tracked 'Big Willie', put through his paces at Hatfield. He was a slow, clumsy creature with a maximum speed of two miles an hour and two huge cartwheels for steering—the engineers had not then discovered how to slew a tracked vehicle round—but he had passed his tests, and a highly secret order for forty of his kind had been placed.

Churchill begged the Prime Minister to allow tanks to be used only in very large numbers for the first time, so as to achieve the maximum effect of surprise and panic, but on 15th September a mere forty-nine went into action across a sea of mud at the Battle of Thiepval, on the Somme. They acquitted themselves well enough for the Commander-in-Chief, Haig, to report that they had been useful, and the German generals do not seem to have taken much notice of the advance information so carelessly offered to them.

In December 1916, Lloyd George became Prime Minister. Churchill was confident that he would be given a Cabinet post in the Government of his old friend and fellow-campaigner; but it was still a Coalition Government, and the Conservatives had to be satisfied as well as the Liberals. Moreover, the people had not forgotten the Dardanelles disaster.

To Churchill's bitter disappointment, he was not included in the Cabinet. In the following March, however, the Dardanelles Report showed that Asquith and Kitchener were at least as much to blame for the failure of that campaign as Churchill. Lloyd George was able to make him Minister of Munitions in July. It was not a Cabinet post, but it gave him some say in the conduct of the war.

The Cabinet still did not share Churchill's enthusiasm for the tank, but fortunately Lloyd George, as Minister of Munitions, had had several hundred tanks built, and there were some military commanders who were ready to use them as Churchill wished. On 20th November 1917, at Cambrai, the Tank Corps, still known as the 'Heavy Machine Guns', put 378 fighting tanks and 98 auxiliary tanks into the field.

Instead of opening the battle with an artillery bombardment which would have warned the enemy of trouble to come, the tanks moved forward under cover of artillery, followed by Canadian infantry. The Germans either fled in panic or surrendered on the spot. Six miles of trenches, 200 guns and 10,000 prisoners were captured. The German General Ludendorff admitted after the war that great numbers of the monsters suddenly bursting through smoke screens struck such terror into his troops that control of the battle was lost.

As Minister of Munitions Churchill was able to vindicate his faith in 'landships'. He also busied himself with that other war-winning weapon of the future, the aeroplane. As First Lord of the Admiralty he had flown for the first time in 1912, in a seaplane. He claims to have invented the name 'seaplane' for that type of aircraft, as well as the use of the word 'flight' to denote an Air Force unit.

In 1914, when the War Office controlled three-quarters of British air strength, and the Admiralty the rest, Kitchener, as Secretary of State for War, had ordered Churchill to use his planes for the air defence of Britain; but Churchill thought that pottering about the skies above south-east England and the Channel on the chance of sighting a Zeppelin was wasteful and unexciting. A squadron of the Royal Naval Air Service, as Churchill himself had named them, landed at Dunkirk on 27th August 1914, and raided the Zeppelin hangars at Cologne and Friedrichshafen. The R.N.A.S. claimed a score of six Zeppelins, bombed submarine bases near Zeebrugge and carried out artillery observation in a year of crazy gallantry with their rickety early machines.

Now, as Minister of Munitions, Churchill flew to France regularly, and witnessed battles from an observation plane. His pilot was a young officer who had been seriously wounded and shell-shocked at Gallipoli and on the Somme, but was fearless in the air. There were few mechanics or airworthy machines to spare at that hectic stage of the war. Churchill was tempting Providence again.

Once a valve broke when their plane was two thousand feet above the Channel, with the French coast five miles behind them. The grey sea below was deserted, and there were no life-jackets and no rubber dinghies in the flimsy plane. Miraculously, the engine sputtered into life, and the pilot turned back to France, to skim over Cap Gris Nez at a hundred feet and land at Marquise aerodrome. There he was given another shaky craft, in which they crossed the Channel and the English coast without incident. Then came a second engine failure, but they glided between two tall elms, this time with only inches to spare, and landed in a small field.

In March 1918, with Russia out of the war, Germany was able to concentrate all her strength on the Western Front against the depleted English and French. It was planned to bring 300,000 Americans a month to Europe, and in fact there were 2,000,000 in France at the Armistice. The Germans had to strike fast and hard.

They did so. In forty days there were 300,000 British casualties, Paris was threatened again, and there was talk of the French breaking contact with the British. Lloyd George sent Churchill in desperate haste to see Clemenceau, the French Prime Minister. Clemenceau took Churchill to the battlefront, and assured him that the French would reinforce the British. The Allies stood firm, and Germany's last effort lost momentum. An Allied victory was certain from that moment, and on 11th November the Armistice was signed.

CHAPTER IX

Churchill at War with the Problems of Peace

The Coalition Government was elected again a month after the Armistice with three times as many seats as its opponents. Churchill, having won his own seat comfortably, became War Minister, with responsibility for the Air Ministry.

Though the fire that had ravaged Europe for four years had been put out in November, there were still dangerous smoulderings in many parts of the world. It fell largely to Churchill to extinguish them, in England, Russia, the Middle East, Ireland and Turkey; and in every case peace was the result; but his methods were so direct and forceful, and people's memories of Antwerp and the Dardanelles were so fresh, that voices were raised in alarm rather than gratitude.

A clear-headed, energetic organizer was needed at the War Office immediately after the Armistice. The Government had decided that the first men to be released from the armed forces should be those whose work was most essential to peacetime industry—the 'key men'. This seemed to be common sense at the time. The 'key men', however, for the very reason that they were so important in their civilian jobs, had been the last to go into the army. The men who had seen years of hardship, danger and wounds on active service became angry and mutinous as these short-service soldiers began to return to their homes. There were ugly demonstrations outside the War Office, mutiny at Folkestone and riots in other large cities. Across the Channel thousands of British troops rushed to the port of Calais and clamoured to return to England.

It took the new War Minister just a fortnight to work out a more popular plan. Men who had been 'first in' were to be 'first out'. Wound stripes were to hasten a man's discharge. The Army of Occupation in Germany was to be formed from young soldiers who had just finished their training, and pay increases and bonuses were to allay their impatience. Within six months three million men had been demobilized smoothly and without fuss.

Churchill is at his best with the ordinary people of Britain when they need firm but fair direction from above. He believes that it is his duty to give them this direction, and that it is their duty to obey. At such times as the demobilization crisis of late 1918 he wins their affection and gratitude.

On the other hand, he does not see himself as one of the people, and has never pretended to. He does not believe that Jack is as good as his master, and he has been a lifelong enemy of British Socialism because he sees it as a step on the road to that most extreme form of Socialism which is called Communism. Before the Armistice of 1918 he was convinced that civilization was threatened by a more terrible scourge than German militarism.

Russia had been our ally from the beginning of the war until the Czar was overthrown by the Bolshevik revolutionaries in 1917. In March 1918, the Bolsheviks made peace with the Germans, and thereby dealt a severe blow to the Allies, since the Russian front had kept a million Germans busy. The Russian armies, loyal to the Czar, continued to hold out in southern and eastern Russia after the revolutionaries had established a government in Moscow.

Were the Allies bound in honour to help them? Churchill had no doubt that they were. For months he attacked the Russian revolutionaries in speech after speech. Socialists and their sympathizers in Britain, however, remembering the Czarist tyranny that the Bolsheviks had overthrown, were unconvinced; and non-Socialists, weary of war, preferred to leave the Russians to solve their own problems.

Finally Churchill went to Paris to ask the Allied Supreme Council for authority to help the Czarist Russians against the Bolsheviks. Lloyd George and the American President, Wilson, gave him a vague answer—vague enough for Churchill to send vast amounts of war material to Russia, and to call for 8,000 volunteers to cover the evacuation of British troops from the north Russian port of Archangel.

People in Britain watched these developments uneasily, but there was a happier ending than many expected; the British withdrawal was successful, and the final defeat of the Czarists in 1920 meant that there could be no further military adventures in Russia, though Churchill supplied the Poles with arms when they unsuccessfully attacked Russia.

In May 1920, a Labour Party group brought back from Russia a document which, they claimed, was an account of an interview between a Russian colonel, Golvin, and Churchill, in which the latter had promised to postpone the evacuation and garrison Archangel with 12,500

3a. With General Montgomery in Normandy, 12th June 1944

3b. At Yalta with President Roosevelt and Marshal Stalin,
9th February 1945

4. Churchill broadcasting the news of Germany's surrender

volunteers. Churchill protested hotly that the paper was a forgery.

At the beginning of the next year he became Colonial Secretary, as he had become War Minister, in time to solve urgent and knotty problems that had defeated others.

The Arabs had fought bravely for us against the Turks during the war, but now the bigger nations at the Paris Peace Conference were trying to bully them out of the share of the Turkish Empire that had been promised to them. The new Colonial Secretary rushed to Cairo and took advice from that other remarkable man, Lawrence of Arabia. The result was justice for the Arabs, who settled down so peacefully that the British Army garrison in Arabia was replaced by an R.A.F. force which cost £35,000,000 a year less.

In Ireland the desperate and ruthless Sinn Fein party had taken over from the cooler-headed Irish Nationalists the struggle to drive out the English. An army of adventurers and ruffians, called the 'Black-and-Tans' from the colours of their uniforms, was sent from England to crush them. The brutal methods of the Black-and-Tans made the Irish so angry and the English so ashamed that the Secretary for Ireland had to resign. Churchill, as Colonial Secretary, was chairman of a Cabinet Committee on Ireland which, by patient talk and cool-tempered bargaining, made Southern Ireland a Dominion and gave her a government strong enough to rule the country.

It was not by quiet reasoning, however, that Churchill settled the strife between Greece and Turkey. After the war Lloyd George had over-generously given most of Turkey's European territory to Greece. A defeated nation that feels that it has been harshly treated at the end of a war often looks for a strong leader who promises to win back its pride and its power; in Turkey there arose the tough and utterly ruthless dictator Kemal Ataturk, who in 1922 fell upon the Greeks and defeated them decisively, burning, pillaging and slaughtering. Everyone believed that he would cross the Dardanelles, the shores of which were occupied by British, French and Italian troops.

Churchill appealed to the Dominions on 15th September to defend the Dardanelles zone, and declared that Britain would bar Kemal's crossing by any means. The French and Italians took fright and left the zone. At home both Conservatives and Socialists condemned Churchill for trying to force the Empire into a new war, and the Government fell. Yet the result of his resolute note to Turkey was that Kemal Ataturk halted his advance short of the British garrison, and a permanent peace was made in November.

When Dundee was called upon to choose its M.P. again in 1922, most people there felt that Churchill's taste for violent action during and after the war had been very un-Liberal. He had no chance to win them back with his charm and his persuasive tongue, for he was rushed to hospital with appendicitis just before his election campaign began. Dundee voted overwhelmingly against him. He wrote jokingly years later that he was left 'without an office, without a seat, without a party, and even without an appendix'.

In the years when the Socialists were gradually taking the place of the Liberals as the chief opponents of the Conservatives, Churchill had no Liberal plans to offer his audiences—only attacks on the Socialists. The result was that the Socialists saw him as their most powerful enemy, the Conservatives still hated him as a deserter from their ranks, and his own Liberals mistrusted him. Twice more he failed to get back into Parliament. It was by sheer luck that he was swept back on a tide of anti-Socialist feeling in 1924—and into high office.

The Foreign Office published a letter said to be an appeal from the Russian Bolsheviks to the British Communists to lead a revolution in Britain. The Labour Party protested that the Conservatives had written the letter themselves, but the people took fright and voted the Conservatives comfortably into power. Churchill, the notorious anti-Socialist, was elected a 'Constitutionalist' Member for Epping, and, to everyone's surprise, including his own, he was offered the Cabinet post of Chancellor of the Exchequer by the Prime Minister, Stanley Baldwin.

The new Chancellor presented his first Budget on 28th April 1925, in a brilliant and amusing way, but Labour and Liberal Members were quick to complain that it favoured the richer people by reducing higher rates of income-tax. Yet at the time politicians of all parties approved of another measure in this Budget which was to bring to the country the worst economic disaster it had ever known. This was the decision to return to the Gold Standard.

After the First World War, with its costly armaments, its destruction and its waste, Britain found herself much poorer than before. Moreover, while most of the country's workers were in the armed forces or engaged in war work of some kind, fewer ordinary goods were made. Because goods were scarce, they became dearer, and wages had to be raised to enable people to live. The higher wages paid to workers meant that prices of the goods they produced were raised still further, and wages had to rise ever higher and higher, without making those who drew them any richer.

Before the war the pound sterling had had the same

value as a fixed amount of pure gold—the amount of gold, in fact, in a sovereign. Since no one can snatch millions of pounds worth of gold out of the air, the higher wages were paid in pound notes and ten-shilling notes—bits of printed paper with no value of their own.

In 1925 the pound would buy only as much as eighteen shillings had done in 1914. This did not matter to an Englishman shopping in England, since he was being paid one pound for every eighteen shillings he had earned in 1914; but it did matter, and very seriously, to an Englishman who bought goods, or gold, abroad, because he was given only eighteen shillings' worth for his pound.

Ever since the end of the war the Government had been gradually reducing the amount of money in circulation in an effort to restore the value of the pound. Now, in his 1925 Budget, Churchill proposed to fix the pound at its former world value in pure gold, and nearly everyone approved his decision.

A young Cambridge economist named J. M. Keynes, however, pointed out that unless the world price of gold suddenly jumped, by sheer good luck, he would be asking foreigners to pay a pound for eighteen shillings' worth of the goods we sent abroad. Before the manufacturer could charge eighteen shillings for eighteen shillings' worth of goods, he would have to reduce the wages of his workers. Later, when most of the British people had been unable, for a considerable time, to buy the things they needed, and when the lowest-paid had suffered poverty and distress, prices would fall and hardship would be relieved, if it had not already caused rioting and revolution.

Keynes' prophecy was first proved accurate in the coal-mining industry, which had been limping along, hardly paying its way, since the war. The price of the coal we sent abroad had to be reduced, and the miners were asked to accept lower wages. They struck, and workers in other industries struck in sympathy. The General Strike began on 4th May 1926, leaving the country virtually without transport, gas, electricity or newspapers.

In calling the General Strike the trade unions had acted against the constitution. The upper and middle classes therefore saw it as their duty to keep the life of the country going by answering the Home Secretary's call for volunteers to drive locomotives and lorries, with military escorts to protect them for the strikers, and to act as special police.

The owner of the *Morning Post* lent Churchill his offices and presses, and Lord Beaverbrook supplied three typesetters, for the publication of a newspaper, the *British Gazette*, containing anti-strike propaganda. The trade unions retorted with a propaganda sheet called the *British Worker*. Here was conflict, and Churchill openly revelled in it. The circulation of the *Gazette* rose from a quarter of a million to two and a quarter million in eight days. The dynamic editor called on the Automobile Association to provide cars to distribute the papers, and brought the crew of a submarine from Devonport to tend the machines. To enter the building one had to show a mauve pass issued by the Treasury.

Against these powerful forces the trade unions could not carry on the General Strike, which ended after nine days. The miners stayed out for another six months, until starvation drove them to complete surrender. The cost to the country was £800,000,000, far higher than the price of a reasonable settlement of the miners' grievances.

A general election was due in 1929. The country had recovered from its misfortunes enough by then for Churchill to present a Budget in April of that year which was calculated to make him more popular with ordinary people than his first Budget had done. It reduced tea prices, railway fares and the cost of motor-cycle licences, and removed a tax on betting. A month later the Prime Minister called for a general election.

The last-minute 'Prosperity Budget' failed, however, to take away the bitter taste of the 1926 struggle or make people forget the widespread unemployment and the niggardly doles and pensions. The Labour Party won 289 seats, the Conservatives 260 and the Liberals 58, and as the ambitions and beliefs of the Labour Party and the Liberals were similar at that time, they joined forces to form a government.

Churchill was out of office again, and was destined to remain so for ten years, like a bound Gulliver helplessly watching the muddling and self-seeking of Lilliputian politicians.

The twenties, not the most successful years of Churchill's political career, were among the most satisfying from other points of view. *The World Crisis*, a vast history of the years 1911–18, appeared volume by volume between 1923 and 1929, and the proceeds, about £20,000, enabled him to buy Chartwell Manor, a country house with a small estate, near Westerham, in a lovely part of Kent.

In 1928 he was registered as an adult apprentice bricklayer in the Amalgamated Union of Building Trade Workers (to the indignation of the union, who thought the joke was in bad taste), and became an accomplished builder. He erected a large part of two cottages on the estate, and built a swimming bath and a goldfish pond. Somehow he found time to work with his four young children on less permanent constructions; he built them a house in the trees, and spent hours with them damming the lake and making waterfalls, returning to the house as wet and muddy as the children themselves.

In 1930 he published a book which reflects the domestic happiness of this time. *My Early Life* traces the author's career from birth to 1908, when, in the last words of the book, he 'married and lived happily ever afterwards'. It is written with a lightness of touch and a delicate, self-mocking humour very different from the ponderous, rolling style of his more important works.

On Sunday afternoon during the war, after he had been replaced as First Lord of the Admiralty and before he decided to serve on the Western Front, Churchill had borrowed a box of colours from one of his children and had tried his hand at painting. He discovered immediately the satisfaction it gave, but he was a timid painter until the wife of a famous artist, Sir John Lavery, showed him how to wield his brush fearlessly and apply the paint more generously. The bold strokes and lavishly applied colour of his better-known paintings show how well he learned the lesson.

Churchill's paintings are mainly of landscapes, sometimes of the quietly beautiful Kentish scene, but more often of the vivid colours and brilliant sunlight of the South of France or Morocco. They have not the practised accuracy of professional work, in detail or perspective, but they have, as one would expect, abundant energy and purpose; and in the thirties he proved that he was a serious painter, and not a mere spare-time dauber relying on his fame in other spheres to attract comment on his work, by exhibiting and selling paintings in Paris under the pseudonym of 'Charles Morin'.

The most important private work of the thirties, however, was the writing of the life of the first Duke of Marlborough. Churchill had been fascinated since boyhood by the handsome and dashing military genius, and at the same time disgusted by the other side of the Duke's nature as portrayed by his favourite historian, Macaulay—his treachery, and the avarice that tempted him into ignoble conduct. Armed with evidence that Macaulay had been unjust to his great ancestor, Churchill undertook the work as a chivalrous struggle against a wicked detractor. With access to unpublished information in Blenheim Palace, he called on historians and military experts to help him, and even visited the scenes of Marlborough's victories on the Continent. The result is a story that takes its energy from Winston Churchill's desire for justice as well as from Marlborough's campaign for power; but its title, *Marlborough: His Life and Times*, is exact, for the book is also a splendid and readable survey of a period of history crowded with remarkable figures.

CHAPTER X

The Thirties: Crying 'Wolf!' in Earnest

In 1929 the prosperity that America had been enjoying since the war suddenly gave way to terrible depression, and millions were thrown out of work. The shock waves of the American crash soon hit Europe and Britain, and the plaintive song of the American ex-soldier reduced to street begging—'Buddy, can you spare a dime?'—was heard in English accents.

A 'National Government' was formed in Britain to deal with the problems of the depression. Ramsay MacDonald, the Labour Prime Minister of the old Government, stayed in office, but promised that the new Government would break up without an election as soon as the trouble was over.

Not only did this National Government reduce the money spent on roads, hospitals, schools, and dole for the unemployed, but it abandoned the gold standard to which Churchill had hoisted the pound, with such painful results, in 1925. Finally, and most disgracefully, MacDonald broke his promise and held a general election. The National Government won, the the Conservatives held most of the seats and all the power. MacDonald, the leader of the Labour Party, stayed on shamelessly as Prime Minister.

A month after this election the Japanese Army seized power in Manchuria, a province of China. Although Britain belonged to the League of Nations, members of which were sworn to band together to defeat an attack on any of its members, all the MacDonald Government did was to forbid the sending of arms to Japan—and to China!

The world's bullies noted the feebleness of the British Government and the easy success of the Japanese aggression, and knew what to do when the Disarmament Conference opened at Geneva a few months later. The only hope of lasting peace lay in all nations disarming completely, but each nation represented at the conference insisted on keeping its pet types of weapons and discarding those it could fight a war without. Germany, disarmed as the chief defeated nation after the war, declared in 1933 that if the others did not disarm, she would re-arm, and withdrew from the Disarmament Conference and the League of Nations.

In fact, Germany had been looking for ways of winning back her old military power ever since the end of the war. Her conquerors had forbidden her to have an army of more than 100,000 men, but she had taken good care that those 100,000 were outstandingly able, the officers of a much larger army of the future. Quiet men in sober suits, working in government departments with innocent-sounding names, were to provide the general staff of this army, and youths and ex-servicemen, training in 'clubs' and 'guilds' of all kinds, were to form the rank and file. Ex-officers of the air force controlled the Civil Aviation Department. Aero and gliding clubs made hundreds of ordinary people into flyers. Crews were trained abroad for secretly built submarines. Material from the war was stored in hidden dumps all over Germany, while factory machinery was specially designed to be easily converted to producing munitions.

At the same time a young man named Adolf Hitler was rising to fame as a public speaker and political organizer. Like the German nation, he was clever and ambitious, and believed that he had been harshly treated. He had come to Vienna before the war to find fame as a painter of pictures, but he had been thankful to find work as a painter and decorator of houses, for he was often out of work, and sometimes hungry. It was as an army corporal, lying in hospital gassed and temporarily blinded, that he learned of Germany's surrender in 1918. He could not believe that Germany had been beaten in a fair fight, and convinced himself that she had been betrayed by Jews and rotted by Communism.

Before Hitler was discharged from the army, his frenzied speeches at meetings of the German Workers' Party were beginning to attract attention, and by 1921 he was the party leader, with a private army of toughs known as 'Storm Troopers' to deal with interference from Communists. The German Workers soon changed their name to 'National Socialists', a clumsy title that was immediately shortened to 'Nazis' in conversation and in newspaper reports. Hitler tried to seize power in Bavaria, in southern Germany, in 1923, and was sentenced to four years' imprisonment, but he was already so popular that he served only thirteen months. During his imprisonment he poured his philosophy of hatred, violence, and nonsense about the purity of the German race into a book called *Mein Kampf*—'My Struggle'—which appeared two years later.

Each succeeding election gave the Nazis more seats in the Reichstag, the German Parliament, and swelled the numbers and power of the Storm Troopers, until the aged

President Hindenburg was glad to accept Hitler as the future Chancellor of Germany in return for some control over his brown-shirted army of bullies. As soon as he became Chancellor in 1933, Hitler disarmed his most powerful rivals, the Communists, and forbade them to hold meetings. The burning down of the Reichstag a month later gave him an excuse to arrest 4,000 Communists, and frightened the Reichstag members into giving him absolute power for four years.

The Brownshirts had bullied the German people and Government into making Hitler Chancellor. Now that Hitler *was* the Government, he found them a nuisance, and their leader, an old comrade named Roehm, a serious danger to his own power. In June 1934, therefore, Hitler personally arrested Roehm and sent him to Munich to be shot with thousands of his colleagues. At the same time, in Berlin, another of Hitler's earliest supporters, Goering, was having all party members of doubtful loyalty executed on the Chancellor's orders. Between 5,000 and 7,000 were murdered in twenty-four hours. It was clear from that day who was the Fuehrer, the leader of the German people.

Events in Italy since the end of the war had taken a similar course, and indeed had moved more rapidly; a few months before Hitler tried, and failed, to snatch power in Bavaria, Mussolini had led his Fascists in a successful march on Rome and had forced the King of Italy to appoint him leader of the Government. Like Hitler, Mussolini was a man of powerful personality made more ruthless by early hardship and poverty. He used his Blackshirts, as Hitler was to use his Brownshirts, to frighten people and Parliament into giving him absolute power, and once in power he mercilessly stamped out all parties that might oppose his own.

Movements like Nazism and Fascism, which come to power by violence and threats, must continue to promise their supporters new and more glorious victories, or they will lose their popularity. When they are all-powerful in their own countries, they must look for glory abroad. In 1935 Italy, one of the original members of the League of Nations, attacked the East African country of Abyssinia, whose admission to the League she herself had backed. Stanley Baldwin succeeded Ramsay MacDonald as British Prime Minister in the summer of that year, and immediately won an election on a promise to defend Abyssinia, but, once safely in the saddle, his National Government allowed Mussolini to do as he liked.

Churchill's attitude to Mussolini's Italy at this time is not easy to understand. He had visited Mussolini in Rome after the General Strike of 1926, and had been charmed by the Italian dictator's manner and impressed by his campaign against Communism. So powerful was his sympathy with the Mussolini régime that when the Fascist armies entered Abyssinia, he advised the British Government to do no more than France to check them, and admitted that he did not expect France to do much. When Britain declared herself ready to act against the aggressor, however, and to punish her by 'economic sanctions', that is, by refusing to send her essential goods, Churchill gave his support wholeheartedly. It was not his fault that the only goods we denied to the Italians were those that ordinary people needed, and not those with which the Fascist armies were attacking the Abyssinians.

By the Treaty of Locarno in 1925, Germany had agreed not to station any troops west of the Rhine or within thirty miles of its eastern bank. France, Britain, Belgium and Italy signed the treaty. Hitler, having noted the feebleness of Britain and France in dealing with Mussolini, sent troops into German territory west of the Rhine in 1936. There were protests, but nothing was done.

Churchill, out of office and therefore powerless to act directly, tirelessly condemned in public the Government's weakness and uncertainty, and pointed out that every other great nation was arming steadily and with determination. Because of his attitude to the Russian revolutionaries and his habit of describing British Socialists as desperate plotters against the state, many people had come to compare him with the shepherd boy who cried 'Wolf!' when no wolf was about. They did not know that Churchill, now at any rate, was crying 'Wolf!' in earnest.

In 1934 Churchill warned the House of Commons that Germany had found an easy way round the clause in the Treaty of Versailles which had forbidden her to build military aircraft; she was making vast numbers of civil aircraft and gliders, all of such a design that they could be converted into warplanes. Later the same year he was able to give figures to show that Germany would be a match for Britain in air strength within a year, and twice as strong two years after that. Baldwin denied these figures, but a few months later they were brazenly confirmed by Hitler himself.

Baldwin's successor as Prime Minister, Neville Chamberlain, did not invite Churchill to join his Government. Perhaps he was afraid that an appointment for Churchill would offend Hitler or Mussolini, with whom he wished to bargain. Anthony Eden, the Foreign Secretary who had opposed Baldwin's feeble policy on Abyssinia, resigned in February 1938, and Chamberlain conducted foreign policy himself from then onwards.

When Hitler occupied Austria, a month after Eden resigned, Chamberlain protested, but was curtly told to mind his own business. He was too timid to back France outright when she said that she would defend Czecho-Slovakia against aggression; instead, he promised that Britain would assist France if she went to war. 'A large part of our dangers and the dangers of Europe,' Churchill pointed out in May, 'is due to the fact that we did not re-arm in time. It was certainly not through lack of warning, but when we at last began it was only in a half-hearted, ramshackle, confused manner.' Between September 1938 and March 1939, the world watched Hitler taking slice after slice of Czecho-Slovakia, and the elderly British Premier flying on three separate occasions to plead with him. France did nothing.

At last some sort of retort came from Chamberlain. He undertook to help Poland if Hitler should turn upon her, though a glance at the map shows that Britain could do very little for Poland against Germany.

In April 1939, the Italians marched into Albania. Churchill now put aside any sympathy he had had for Mussolini's régime, and his detestation of Russian Communism, and pressed for an agreement with Russia for the defence of Poland. After delays, an approach was made to Russia, not by the Foreign Secretary, but by a junior official of the Foreign Office. Russia wanted France and Britain to commit themselves to defending the Baltic States as well, and Churchill declared this a very reasonable request, but the Russians soon realized that the British mission had not come to negotiate seriously at all, and made a non-aggression pact with Hitler.

Hitler invaded Poland on 1st September. Public anger prevented Chamberlain from pleading with him again through Mussolini the following day. On the morning of the 3rd, British radio listeners heard his gravelly voice announce that we were at war with Germany.

CHAPTER XI

At the Admiralty Again:
the 'Phoney War'

Now that we were at war, many British people felt as though a weight had been lifted from their minds. This is not as strange as it might seem; for years they had watched successive governments yielding tamely to the demands of bullies abroad, and they knew that the longer war was postponed, the more powerful would those bullies become.

About an hour after the declaration of war, Churchill was appointed to the same office of First Lord of the Admiralty that he had held at the beginning of the First World War. At the Admiralty he called for, and was given, the map on which he had traced the movements of ships in 1914. He worked into the small hours, and was back at his desk at ten the next morning.

If the appointment of Churchill to the Admiralty showed that the British Government meant business at last, it was obvious all too soon that the enemy meant business too. A few hours after the declaration of war the liner *Athenia* was torpedoed 200 miles west of Ireland with 1,400 passengers, 300 of them Americans. Hitler's Propaganda Minister, Dr. Goebbels, tried to deflect American anger by blaming Churchill!

The First Lord of the Admiralty did not start the Second World War, as he had done the first, with Britannia complacently ruling the waves; within a fortnight the Germans sank over a hundred thousand tons of our shipping and many ships belonging to neutral countries; the old aircraft carrier *Courageous* went down trying to protect unarmed and unconvoyed ships hurrying home after the outbreak of war; a German submarine sneaked into the harbour of Scapa Flow and torpedoed the battleship *Royal Oak*; and the armed merchant cruiser *Rawalpindi* went blazing to the bottom after a one-sided fight with the pocket battleship *Deutschland*.

Luckily, the picture had its other side. Without delay Churchill devised a convoy system by which merchant ships sailed in large numbers escorted by naval vessels, and set the navy to capturing German merchant ships. Within a month the enemy's shipping losses were much higher than our own, and by the end of the year he had lost half his submarines. The British cruisers *Ajax*, *Exeter* and *Achilles* forced the vastly more powerful pocket battleship *Graf Spee* to take refuge at Montevideo, in Uruguay, after a furious battle, and compelled her captain to avoid further shame by scuttling her and taking his own life. 'In a dark, cold winter,' Churchill commented on this heroic action, 'it warmed the cockles of the British heart.' In February 1940, H.M.S. *Cossack* attacked the German prison-ship *Altmark* in a Norwegian fjord, and with the shout, 'The navy's here!' her boarding party freed 299 British prisoners who had been locked in storerooms and a disused oil tank.

At sea, then, in the first months of the war, the sparks flew, as they tend to do where Churchill is closely concerned. On land, the resistance of the Poles to the Nazi invaders had ceased after a fortnight, and Hitler's

G   97

armoured columns had probed beyond Warsaw. At that point Russian troops occupied eastern Poland. Hitler now dared to turn to the Allies and ask them to make peace, since they had gone to war over Poland, and Poland no longer existed!

Meanwhile the British Expeditionary Force in France was engaged in what the news bulletins called 'patrol activity'. There was no serious attempt to engage the enemy. The R.A.F., to its own disgust, was bombarding Germany—with leaflets. Parallel to the Maginot Line, the elaborate and costly system of defences along France's frontier with Germany, the Germans were building their own Siegfried Line, and could work throughout the night by floodlight, secure in the knowledge that the French and British would not attack or bomb them.

Fortunately the morale of the people at home was buoyed up in October 1939, by the first of those Churchillian broadcasts which are now a part of world history. The First Lord condemned the Nazis and their leader in the strongest terms, and appealed to neutral countries to join England and France in the fight instead of hoping to buy safety by yielding to Hitler's wishes.

Churchill was not yet, of course, the leader of the nation, but the bewildered people were turning more and more for inspiration to the man who was fighting a brilliant war at sea and who could rouse them with such lively and often humorous turns of phrase.

In mid-April the Prime Minister, reassured by the fact that the German armies had done nothing spectacular since the invasion of Poland, was bold enough to venture a Churchillian figure of speech; Hitler, he said, had 'missed the bus'.

Five days later German forces landed in all the important harbours of Norway, sailed into Oslo and Copenhagen, and drove up through Denmark in the slickest and most ruthless combined operation yet witnessed. Churchill demanded a frontal assault on Trondheim, the important port in the centre of Norway, which was weakly held, but Chamberlain was too timid, and before a cautious pincer movement could close on the port from north and south, a strong German force had thrust up the country by land to Trondheim. Up in the north, at Narvik, a British force of 20,000 was held off by 6,000 Germans for weeks. Within eight weeks of the first British landings all our troops had been taken off again.

The mood of Parliament was bitter and resentful when the Norwegian campaign was debated. L. S. Amery (of the swimming-bath incident at Harrow) addressed to Chamberlain the brutally blunt words used by Oliver Cromwell three centuries earlier in dissolving his Long Parliament: 'You have sat too long here for any good you have been doing. Depart, I say, and let us have done with you! In the name of God, go!'

If Amery was blunt, Lloyd George, who had led the country with such vigour in the First World War, was cutting. 'There is nothing,' he said of Chamberlain, 'which can contribute more to victory in this war than that he should sacrifice the seals of office.' When Churchill unselfishly tried to take some of the blame for the recent disasters, Lloyd George asked him not to 'allow himself to be converted into an air-raid shelter to keep the splinters from hitting his colleagues.'

The vote of the House was so overwhelmingly against Chamberlain that he knew the present Government could not continue. He appealed to the Labour leaders the next day to join the administration. Just before dawn the day after that, Friday, 10th May, before the Labour answer came, the Nazis poured into Holland, Belgium and Luxemburg. Now there could be only one answer.

An all-party Ministry was at once formed, with Churchill as Prime Minister and Defence Minister. Within twenty-four hours he had mustered his War Cabinet of five members and the chiefs of the army, navy and air force. He wrote later of this hectic time: 'As I went to bed at about three a.m. I was conscious of a profound sense of relief. At last I had the authority to give directions over the whole scene. I felt as if I were walking with destiny, and that all my past life had been but a preparation for this hour and for this trial.' On the following Monday he told the House in grave tones: 'I have nothing to offer but blood, toil, tears and sweat.' With typical generosity he made Chamberlain a member of his War Cabinet and invited him to continue as leader of the Conservative Party.

CHAPTER XII

Churchill Commands the Besieged Garrison

To check the German advance westward, the British and French advanced into Belgium and Holland. Hitler promptly directed his main spearhead to the south, through the thickly wooded, rugged Ardenne :country. Clouds of paratroopers and savage bombardments of cities brought the Dutch to their knees in four days. The Belgians resisted for seventeen days. The German drive through the Ardennes curled 'like a sharp scythe', in Churchill's words, 'around the right and rear of the armies of the north'. Boulogne and Calais held out for a time, but soon the only way of retreat was by sea from the port of Dunkirk. Churchill expected only 20,000 or 30,000 men to escape.

Miraculously, over 300,000 were ferried to safety in England, through the menace of magnetic mines and U-boats and the dive-bombing of the terrible Stukas, by 220 light warships and a motley fleet of 650 merchant and pleasure craft. As the last men were snatched off the Dunkirk beaches, Churchill delivered a magnificent speech of defiance in the House of Commons: 'We shall defend our island, whatever the cost may be, we shall fight on the beaches, we shall fight on the landing grounds, we shall fight in the fields and in the streets, we shall fight in the hills: we shall never surrender.'

Meanwhile the German armoured columns were roaring down into France behind the useless concrete of the Maginot Line. On 10th June, with France on her knees, Mussolini entered the war on Hitler's side. On the same day the French Premier, Reynaud, in flatter, less stirring phrases, echoed Churchill's determination to fight to the last. But Paris was not defended. The French Government fled to Tours, and soon afterwards to Bordeaux. On 14th June Nazi tanks clattered along the Champs Elysées, and the swastika emblem flew from the top of the Eiffel Tower. The doddering eighty-four-year old Marshal Pétain, a hero of the First World War, but now a Nazi sympathizer made Prime Minister by the conquerors, was ready to hand over the powerful French Fleet to his new masters.

On 3rd July Churchill moved, as always, swiftly and decisively. The British Navy took over all French warships in our ports and ordered those at Alexandria into internment. At Oran, in Algeria, a large and formidable part of the French Navy, including two modern cruisers, the *Dunkerque* and the *Strasbourg*, was confronted with an even stronger British force, the commander of which gave the French the choice of four courses—to join the British, to accept internment in a British port, to cross to Martinique in the French West Indies for internment, or to fight it out. The French Admiral Gensoul chose the last course. For ten minutes there was an exchange of fire between the French vessels and the shore batteries on the one hand, and the British cruisers and naval aircraft from the *Ark Royal* on the other. All the French ships were burnt, sunk or driven ashore except one cruiser, which escaped, heavily damaged, to Toulon.

Churchill became leader of the Conservative Party in

October on Chamberlain's retirement from the War Cabinet. In the following month Chamberlain died, and Churchill paid a generous tribute in Parliament to the man responsible for many of the errors and omissions he had been called upon to put right.

England was now indeed fighting on alone. Churchill broadcast a heartening message to the French people in October in which he spoke of Britain's readiness to repel any attempted invasion. He spoke contemptuously of Mussolini as Hitler's 'little Italian accomplice . . . trotting along, hopefully and hungrily, but rather wearily and very timidly, at his side'.

Hitler perhaps believed that he could finish off the small northern island at his leisure, or even that a merciless pounding from the air for some weeks might bring a British surrender without invasion.

Nothing happened until early August. Then came the attempt to smash our seaports. The air defence was much more stubborn than the Germans had expected. From the 13th until the 23rd the aerodromes of the south and southeast of England suffered the full fury of the Luftwaffe; but on none of these eleven days were the enemy losses less than twice our own; 75 German aircraft and 34 British were destroyed on 15th August alone. On 20th August, Churchill, in one of his finest utterances, praised the young airmen who were thwarting Hitler's invasion plans. 'Never in the field of human conflict,' he said, 'was so much owed by so many to so few.'

From 24th August until 6th September, while the pounding of the southern aerodromes continued by day, Swansea, Bristol and Plymouth in the south-west, Birmingham in the Midlands, and Liverpool and Birkenhead in the north-west were bombed night after night. Our losses were heavier in this phase; 286 of our planes were brought down; but the R.A.F. was far from crippled, and had taken the frightful toll of 380 of the enemy in the same period.

Finally, on 7th September the 'softening-up' of the great cities began with raids on London. On a single day, 15th September, 60 or 70 of the German aircraft that approached the capital were destroyed. August 15th had taught Hitler the bitter lesson that the conquest of the skies over Britain would be a long and costly undertaking; on 15th September he must have recognized defeat. The daylight raids continued through September and October, but the attacks came in at higher and higher levels, and the bombs were less and less accurately aimed.

The Prime Minister shared, as he also inspired, the excitement, the fearless spirit, the cheerfulness and even the humour of this time of national ordeal. He was dissuaded with difficulty from sleeping at 10 Downing Street, but it was his habit to watch and listen to the flash and roar of ack-ack guns and exploding bombs at night from the roof of the Government 'annexe' at Storey's Gate, near St. James's Park. The day after a severe raid, Churchill was often to be seen inspecting the stricken areas, chatting and shaking hands with well-wishers, or standing beside Mrs. Churchill in an open car and waving encouragement, until the poignant sight of cheering, smiling people standing in the rubble of their bombed homes overcame him, and he wept openly.

Downing Street, the Storey's Gate 'annexe', and Chequers, the Prime Minister's official country home in the Chilterns, formed the background to Churchill's prodigious volume of work, done at a pace that he expected those around him to match. His devoted secretaries had to adjust themselves to his irregular hours; they had to learn to type his speeches in a peculiar form, with lines of uneven length to mark stresses and pauses, and to alter them when vital news came to hand a few minutes before the Prime Minister was due to broadcast; and they had to learn to respect a great man's little foibles—his hatred of pins, paper-clips and the rustle of paper!

Gradually, in the spring and summer of 1941, the severity of the raids lessened. Instead of trudging downstairs for a cold, sleepless night in the shelters, the people heard the warning sirens and stayed in their beds, confident that the 'all-clear' signal would not be long delayed.

Profiting from the fact that Britain stood alone against the German onslaught, Mussolini now dominated the Mediterranean, which he referred to as 'an Italian lake'. The little British island of Malta was bombed, and from their own African empire the Italians invaded British possessions in East Africa. They attacked Greece on 28th October, and, greatly to their surprise, were thrown back.

Churchill, seeing a Mediterranean passage denied to him, sent a force equipped with tanks to Egypt via the Cape, and called Australian and New Zealand troops to his aid. In November a Fleet Air Arm raid on the Italian harbour of Taranto put important Italian naval units out of the war. A fortnight later twenty Italian planes flew up the Thames to bomb London. Challenged by Spitfires, they flew for their lives without having dropped a single bomb on the capital. Only thirteen returned to Italy.

The following month General Wavell started a victorious push through Egypt and Libya, and Churchill broadcast an appeal to the Italian people which cleverly undermined the tottering authority of their leader. He had an even more heartening tale of success for his radio audience in February—an advance of four hundred miles in North Africa, the capture of a complete Italian army, the conquest of the whole of Cyrenaica, the return of the deposed Emperor of Abyssinia to his native land, and the beginning of a campaign which was to strip the Italians of all their African possessions.

Churchill's references to the 'crafty, cold-blooded, black-hearted Italian' became ever more biting. Germany having come to the Italians' aid in Greece, Mussolini's announcement of a 'victory' there detonated a blast of Churchillian contempt: 'This whipped jackal Mussolini, who to save his own skin has made all Italy a vassal state of Hitler's empire, comes frisking up at the side of the German tiger.'

The successes against the Italians were not the only encouragement for isolated and battered Britain during the months that followed the fall of France. The American President, Roosevelt, voiced the wishes of his nation when, on 10th June, he promised us all the material help the resources of the United States could afford. In September America gave us fifty destroyers in exchange for the lease of certain bases, and at the beginning of 1941 Roosevelt launched the 'Lease-Lend' scheme for the supply of arms and equipment. Churchill's acknowledgement went across the water: 'We shall not fail or falter. We shall not weaken or tire. Neither the sudden shock of battle nor the long-drawn trials of vigilance and exertion will wear us down. Give us the tools and we will finish the job!'

Sadly let down by his 'little Italian accomplice', Hitler set about conquering the Balkans himself. Bulgaria joined him in March without a struggle and allowed his troops passage to the Greek frontier. Then he made a savage onslaught on Greece and Jugoslavia. To meet the threat, Churchill withdrew troops from Wavell in North Africa.

Units of Mussolini's Navy, on orders, no doubt, from

his German master, appeared off the southern tip of Greece, Cape Matapan, to intercept this British expedition. Units of the British Navy appeared there too, with results that we, and perhaps the Italians, had learned to expect. One Italian battleship was crippled and three cruisers and two destroyers sunk, the British ships emerging unharmed.

After a month of desperate fighting we were driven out of Greece and Crete. German troops and armour, thrown into the North African campaign, pushed Wavell's weakened forces eastwards back to Egypt, leaving us only Tobruk of all the coastal towns we had won from the Italians.

On 10th May one of the most extraordinary single incidents of the war took place; Rudolf Hess, Hitler's deputy, dropped by parachute into Scotland, hoping to meet the Duke of Hamilton, through whom it was his intention to arrange an Anglo-German alliance against Russia! Churchill immediately warned Stalin of the imminent German assault of his country. Once again, Hitler's patience was exhausted, and on 22nd June his armoured columns stabbed into Soviet Russia.

Churchill lost no time in telling the nation that, although he had never tried to hide his personal detestation of Communism, Britain would do everything in her power to help the Russians against 'this bloodthirsty guttersnipe', Hitler.

His next important step was to cross the Atlantic in the new battleship, the *Prince of Wales*, to meet the American President in Placentia Bay, Newfoundland. From this meeting emerged the Atlantic Charter, an eight-point declaration making clear to the world the democratic ideals we were fighting for. A message was sent to the Russian leader, Stalin, suggesting a meeting in Moscow.

The Moscow Conference was held on 24th August, within a week of Churchill's return from Newfoundland; Britain and America offered Russia unstinted help in the fight against Hitler.

Though he repeatedly announced that resistance to his latest aggression was at an end, Hitler soon realized that his armies would have to spend the winter in Russia. In Africa his once-victorious troops were being thrown back. American materials of all kinds were being rushed across the Atlantic. But he still had a card to play.

On 7th December 1941, while the Japanese envoy Kurusu was in Washington promising peaceful relations between his country and America, Japanese aircraft and submarines attacked and crippled the American Pacific Fleet at its base at Pearl Harbour, Hawaii, and bombed American-held islands in the Pacific. Britain declared war on Japan the next day, and Hitler and Mussolini declared war on America on the two succeeding days.

When Churchill addressed the American Congress on 26th December he spoke encouragingly of the Allies' prospects for 1942 and 1943, and with indignation of the Japanese treachery. 'What kind of a people do they think we are?' he demanded. There was need of stirring language like this, for the Japanese had sunk the *Prince of Wales* and the *Repulse*, and were leap-frogging from one Pacific island to another. They had landed in the Philippines, and Hong Kong had fallen to them on Christmas Day, the day before Churchill's speech.

A few days later he spoke to the Canadian Parliament in Ottawa. He recalled how, as France fell, the defeatist French General Weygand had forecast that in three weeks England would have her neck wrung like a chicken. 'Some chicken,' growled Churchill to the Canadians, 'and some neck!'

The first half of 1942 was the blackest period of the war. The German warships *Scharnhorst, Gneisenau* and *Prinz Eugen* sailed through the Channel from Brest to German waters. The Japanese took Singapore and Rangoon, and were hammering at the gates of India. The Germans in Russia resumed their advance towards Stalingrad and the southern oilfields, and simultaneously Rommel of the German Afrika Korps began a drive eastwards through Cyrenaica which was destined to be halted only at El Alamein, just short of Alexandria. Our only counter-stroke in these grim months was the ever-heavier bombing of German cities; it was in the otherwise gloomy month of May that the first 1,000-bomber raids were made on Hamburg and Bremen.

While Churchill was paying another visit to Roosevelt in America, the news reached England that Tobruk had fallen to the Germans, with 25,000 troops and a great amount of material. He returned to face bitter criticism in Parliament and in the country—criticisms of the disasters in Libya and the failure to open a second front in Europe. He could not reassure the people by revealing the purpose of his latest American journey, the planning of an Anglo-American landing in North Africa.

A few weeks later Churchill was travelling again, this time to Cairo, to nominate what was to prove an unbeatable team—General Alexander as Commander-in-Chief, Middle East, and General Montgomery as Commander of the Eighth Army. From Cairo and Persia he flew on to Moscow to explain to Stalin why the British and Americans could not yet open the second front which would drain German strength away from the sorely pressed Russian defences.

Each of these great leaders heartily disliked the form of government and way of life that the other represented, but they had a good deal in common as individuals; they enjoyed good food and drink, and conversation into the small hours of the morning; they both loved power, and wielded it with enormous energy; they had both led adventurous lives; and both appreciated plain speaking. Though it was hard, as Churchill explained to Parliament on his return, to make the Russians see the technical difficulties of launching a full-scale landing in Europe, Churchill and Stalin parted on good terms.

CHAPTER XIII

The Defenders Sally Out

Alexander's and Montgomery's genius in North Africa turned the tables completely on the formidable Rommel within ten days in October 1942, and tens of thousands of Germans surrendered or fled in utter rout. British and American troops poured ashore a few days later in Algeria and Morocco, where the French supporters of the Pétain Government tamely yielded to them.

At Stalingrad, not merely had the garrison not surrendered, but a huge Russian pincer movement had closed round the 300,000 German besiegers, and when the German Field-Marshal von Paulus disobeyed Hitler's orders and raised the white flag in January 1943, only 12,000 of them were left alive.

A conference was held at Casablanca in the same month between Churchill, Roosevelt and General de Gaulle, leader of the Free French, to take stock of the war on all fronts, and to agree on harrying the Germans to unconditional surrender. How much more heartening this meeting must have been than those that had gone before it!

Churchill developed pneumonia on his return to England in February, and Mrs. Churchill and the doctors managed to persuade him to deal only with the most important state papers. At this time a well-wisher presented him with a magnificent lion named Rota. The invalid showed a photograph of the beast, with its jaws gaping, to an assistant secretary, a rather small man, warning him that if his work was not satisfactory he would be fed to Rota, as meat was very scarce. The secretary, alarmed not for himself but for his master, reported that the Prime Minister was delirious!

As if to make up for these weeks when he was able to do only three men's work instead of ten, Churchill spent the rest of 1943 travelling and conferring and speaking and working as never before.

He addressed the United States Congress in Washington in May, and began the planning of 'Operation Overlord', the long-awaited opening of the second front, with Roosevelt. The last time he had visited America the news of the German capture of Tobruk had followed him; this time he was told of the surrender of the German Army in Tunisia.

Back in London, in the bomb-shattered Guildhall, he hinted at a major action in the Mediterranean in autumn, and within a few days the Allies landed in Sicily. They took only five weeks to capture the whole island, but by then Churchill had crossed the Atlantic again, and was concerting plans for 'Overlord' with Roosevelt in Canada.

The following month the Allies landed on the mainland of Italy. Mussolini had been overthrown by his countrymen, who now hurried to lay down their arms, but the Germans fought on in the Apennines.

1943 ended with a series of historic meetings of heads of states. In November Churchill and Roosevelt met in Cairo. After Cairo came the first meeting of the three giants, Churchill, Roosevelt and Stalin, at Teheran, in an

Arabian-Nights setting against the background of the snow-clad Elbruz mountains. It was here that Churchill presented the Russian leader with a sword in honour of the defenders of Stalingrad, the gift of King George VI.

The fairy-tale surroundings and gracious ceremony of Teheran did not preclude serious business. It was decided that British and American forces should land in northern France from England and in southern France from Italy, while Russia was to launch a huge offensive on the eastern front.

From Teheran, where he celebrated his sixty-ninth birthday, Churchill returned to Cairo for talks with Roosevelt and the President of Turkey, and intended to cross to the Italian front, but he fell ill, and on 16th December it was announced that he had pneumonia. It was not until 18th January 1944, after convalescence in French Morocco, that he was able to come home.

Churchill was kept in England during the early months of 1944 by the pressure of preparations for the invasion. As in the First World War, he was not content to leave the details to subordinates; his fertile mind was full of his own and other men's ideas, all ingenious, some fantastic, for ensuring successful landings.

The invasion fleet crossed the Channel on the dark, wet night of 5th June. Parachute and glider-borne troops floated down on the fields behind the coast. The beachheads were established by morning, and the invasion of the Continent was a reality. More than a quarter of a million troops were landed in the first twenty-four hours. Within three days we had our own airfields in France.

Churchill himself was in Normandy six days after the first landings, and spent three days with the Allied troops a month later. From a warship in the Mediterranean he watched the landings in the south of France a fortnight after the invasion of Normandy.

A third bout of pneumonia did not prevent him from conferring with the American President again in Canada in September. The main purpose of the Quebec conference was to plan the downfall of Japan. Britain, America and Canada agreed to pool the results of their atomic research and to keep their secrets from the rest of the world—including Russia.

Meanwhile British troops had burst out of the Normandy beachheads and hammered their way eastwards across northern France, the Free French had entered Paris and the Americans had thrust down across France to the Siegfried Line. The Russians were rolling the Germans back on a front from the Baltic to the Black Sea. As the Soviet tide flooded across their frontiers, Rumania and Bulgaria rounded on their German masters and declared war on them. The resistance leader Tito, later to be President of Jugoslavia, helped by Allied forces from Italy and Russians fresh from Rumania, expelled the Germans from his country. The Germans in Greece, too, withdrew in disorder, and British forces entered Athens in October.

For four years Churchill had focused the full power of his formidable mind and personality on the crushing of Nazism and Fascism. Now that victory was almost certain, he and the other Allied leaders had to think about 'winning the peace'—making sure that the world after the fighting would be a better place than that which Hitler and Mussolini had bullied in the thirties. But the problems of peace have often shown Churchill less sure of himself than those of war.

It was natural that Communists and other Socialists should have played prominent and often heroic parts in the resistance movements of Europe against their archenemies, the Nazi and Fascist conquerors. When the war-time alliance with Russia had served its purpose, however, Churchill's lifelong hatred of Communism led him to take strong action, in Italy, Greece and Jugoslavia, against movements which had hastened our victory, and to ally himself with anti-Communists whose own records in the service of freedom were doubtful.

In Poland, on the other hand, Churchill went to such extraordinary lengths to please his Russian ally that he was criticized by Conservatives and supported by Labour M.P.s. In early 1944 Stalin demanded territory which had been Polish at the outbreak of war. The exiled Polish Government in London refused. Churchill then revealed that he had already agreed with Stalin that Russia should take parts of Poland, and that Poland should be given parts of Germany in return. This 'carving-up' of Poland, as many people disapprovingly called it, was confirmed at the Yalta Conference, and the British Government ceased to recognize the Polish refugee Government that tried to prevent it.

In France, a country that Churchill has always loved, the post-war settlement went more smoothly. De Gaulle included representatives of the French resistance move-ment in his new Government, which was immediately recognized by Britain, America and Russia. Churchill himself made a triumphal return to Paris on Armistice Day, and walked down the Champs Elysées to the cheers of the French crowds who had listened secretly to his broadcasts in the darkest days of the German occupation. He was made a freeman of Paris the following day, and spoke to the French people, expressing the modest hope that his bad French would not shake the alliance!

Churchill, Roosevelt and Stalin met again at Yalta in

February 1945. The once-beautiful Crimean resort of the czars and noblemen of old Russia was in a state of ruin that deeply shocked the Western visitors. Besides the fixing of the new Polish frontiers, the aim of the meeting was to agree on the matter-of-fact business behind the cheers and flag-waving of the impending victory, how the states freed from Nazi domination were to be governed, and how future wars were to be prevented by a world security organization.

It was obvious to everyone who saw him at this meeting that Roosevelt was physically very sick, and, perhaps because he knew that his influence would not be effective much longer, very sick at heart for the future of the world. He did not like the chopping about of the frontiers of Poland, and the idea of the great powers haggling for 'spheres of influence' in Europe, instead of leaving countries to govern themselves, dismayed him.

Nevertheless Yalta was acclaimed throughout the free world as a great triumph, and the Big Three parted on terms of the warmest cordiality. Churchill flew on to Athens and the Middle East, and came home to tell the House of Commons of the absolute necessity of living on friendly terms with the Russians. A few days later Roosevelt collapsed and died.

Meanwhile the Allied armies crossed the Rhine and thrust into Germany. Churchill was in Germany himself a month after Yalta, firing towards the German lines a huge shell bearing a chalked personal message for Hitler, crossing the Rhine with Eisenhower, the Allied Supreme Commander, and Montgomery, and narrowly escaping enemy shelling. In April American and Russian forces met and shook hands on German soil.

In the same month Mussolini was caught as he tried to flee to Switzerland and executed by Italian partisans. A million Germans surrendered to Field Marshal Alexander's forces in Italy a few days later. Holland, Denmark and Austria were liberated in early May, and Hitler and other Nazi leaders committed suicide.

In one of his most moving broadcasts, and deeply moved by the occasion himself, Churchill told the world on 8th May of the unconditional surrender of all German forces. As he made his way towards Parliament he was mobbed by delirious crowds. Parliament rose to pay him tribute. He thanked them and led them to St. Margaret's Church, Westminster, to give thanks to God for deliverance. Wildly cheering, singing admirers acclaimed him when he appeared on a balcony in Whitehall in the evening.

He had accomplished the task for which destiny had preserved him through an adventurous and turbulent youth, and to which destiny had called him at an age when most ordinary men retire from active life.

CHAPTER XIV

The Veteran Warrior and the New Problems of Peace

The Conservative and Labour Parties were both eager to have done with the Coalition Government in which they had joined forces five years earlier. Churchill resigned as Prime Minister on 23rd May and was immediately reappointed to lead the three-week caretaker Government which was to act until the general election.

After nearly half a century of parliamentary life, Churchill still saw party politics as a game, an aristocratic game of skill in winning over the voters by painting one's own side snow-white and one's opponents' pitch-black. In all the lurid terms he had used to condemn the Russian Bolsheviks at the end of the First World War, and the British Socialists in the early twenties, he now attacked the Labour Party and its leaders, sober and for the most part elderly citizens who had served him so ably and faithfully in the wartime coalition. He charged Attlee, Morrison, Bevin and their like with plotting to establish a police state and enslave their fellow-countrymen.

Churchill's audiences in the Midlands, the North and the Lowlands of Scotlands listened with delight and the affection due to the man who had led the country to victory; but they had already decided how they were going to vote. Civilian Britain went to the polls on 5th July. As the count was not to be made for three weeks to allow the servicemen to vote, Churchill went off confidently to the south of France for a holiday, and from there to Potsdam for the last wartime meeting of the Allied leaders.

When the votes were counted it was found that Labour had won twice as many seats as the Conservatives. Attlee took Churchill's place as Prime Minister and representative of Britain at Potsdam. Churchill did not hide his disappointment; at the end of the first volume of *The Second World War* he wrote bitterly: 'All our enemies having surrendered unconditionally or being about to do so, I was immediately dismissed by the British electorate from all further conduct of their affairs.'

Japan, indeed, was very close to unconditional surrender. The victorious sweep through the islands of the Pacific, through Malaya, Siam and Burma, had stretched her lines of communication to snapping point. Her fighting soldiers were better than the industrial system that armed and supplied them. Against the American weapons and war material of all kinds that poured into the war in south-east Asia, they were driven on to the defensive. Desperate stands like those at Kohima and Imphal in Assam in mid-1944 ended in Japanese retreat, and in the next year defeat turned into rout. The Japanese garrisons of the Pacific islands were winkled out painfully one by one.

Churchill and the new American President, Truman, were at Potsdam, agreeing on plans for landings in Japanese-held Malaya, the Dutch East Indies and Japan itself, when they were told that atomic bomb tests in Mexico had been successful. They immediately decided to use the new weapon against Japan. Atomic bombs were dropped on the crowded factory towns of Hiroshima and Nagasaki. Nearly a quarter of a million people were killed, or have since died from the effects of radiation, in Hiroshima alone. Churchill's excuse for this terrible decision was that it saved millions of Allied lives by forcing Japan to surrender immediately, but we know now that the Japanese were begging to lay down their arms before the bombs were dropped. Why, then, did Churchill and Truman give the order?

Russia declared war on the stunned and beaten Japanese two days after the atom-bombing. Many people condemned Russia, as they had condemned Italy for declaring war on France in 1940, for joining in a fight when the enemy was already on his knees. In fact, Churchill had agreed with Stalin before the end of the war in Europe that Russia should declare war on Japan three months after the surrender of the Germans. Stalin kept this bargain to the day. It is hard not to believe that the atom bombs were dropped so that the Russian armies would have no chance to pour into Japan as they had flooded across so much of Europe behind the beaten Germans.

On 15th August Mr. Attlee presented the nation's formal congratulations to the King on the defeat of the Japanese.

Freed from the strain of directing the British war effort, and even from the cares of a peacetime Prime Minister, Churchill sought other outlets for his restless energy at Chartwell, where he had bought a 500-acre farm. Some of his finest paintings belong to this period—pictures of Chartwell at different seasons, of the beloved south coast of France and the picturesque gorges of the Maritime Alps. The title of Honorary Academician Extraordinary was invented for him in 1949, and six of his works were hung at the Royal Academy.

In much the same casual, accidental way in which he had taken up his most absorbing hobby of painting when work and responsibility were lighter than usual in 1915, he turned in 1949 to racehorse-owning. He accepted an offer of an inexpensive colt, Colonist II, and registered the chocolate-and-pink colours his father had used. After a poor start, Colonist II won popular victories at Ascot and Windsor, and had a triumphant season in 1950. The Churchill stable was successful with other horses after Colonist II was sold in 1951.

Churchill's most important work outside Parliament at this time was the writing of his history of the Second World War. Not only had he lived and made much of the history he was compiling, but he had the advantage of being able to employ professional historians and experts from the armed services. Dictating thousands of words a day, he published five of the six massive volumes during his time out of office.

During the war the Government had taken over very strict control of the country's factories and businesses so that every scrap of material and every worker's energy would be put to the best use. Clothes and fuel, as well as food, were rationed, and most other goods were hard to get. The Labour Party kept many of these controls after the war, hoping that if we bore our hardships for a few more years we would soon be able to 'stand on our own feet' and not have to borrow from our wealthy American friends.

Churchill knew that the people were sick of these war-time hardships, and that many of them could not understand why they had to bear them in peacetime. Imitating the pre-war slogan of the Hitler Youth Movement, 'Strength through Joy', he called the Labour policy

'Strength through Misery', and the people laughed with him. They read and listened to his colourful, robust speeches with relish and affection, remembering the part he had played in winning the war; but most of them still believed that Labour had the better plan for 'winning the peace', for they voted for Churchill's opponents when seats in the House of Commons became vacant and new M.P.s had to be elected.

The Labour Government was to find itself in grave financial difficulties in 1949, and Churchill and his party were to have their chance of turning triumphantly to the people and reminding them of these earlier warnings; but for the moment he was not listened to seriously when he talked of financial matters, perhaps because his own poor showing as Chancellor of the Exchequer in the twenties was still remembered. When he talked of foreign affairs, however, his audiences recalled how he had tried in the thirties to awaken the country to the danger from Germany and Italy, and they listened seriously and attentively.

During a visit to America in early 1946, Churchill travelled to address the people of Fulton, in Missouri, after talks in Washington with President Truman. The meeting was unusually well advertised, and the world sensed that his speech would be of special importance.

Having called for an international army to see that the wishes of the United Nations Organization were carried out, Churchill gave thanks that atomic secrets had stayed in American hands, and spoke of the policies of Soviet Russia: 'From Stettin in the Baltic to Trieste in the Adriatic,' he told his audience, 'an iron curtain has descended across the Continent.' All the countries of central and eastern Europe, he complained, were controlled by Moscow. Only Greece was 'free to decide its future at an election under British, American and French observation.

The Russian-dominated Polish Government has been encouraged to make enormous and wrongful inroads upon Germany.' 'I do not believe that Soviet Russia desires war,' he reflected. 'What they desire is the fruits of war and the indefinite expansion of their power and doctrines.'

At first American Democrats and British Labour M.P.s protested hotly, and disagreed with these startling opinions; but the term 'Iron Curtain' passed into the common speech of many languages, and mistrust of Russia spread throughout the non-Communist world. By June the Labour Foreign Secretary was deploring in Parliament the abuse that Moscow was directing at the western countries. 'I would not have believed it possible,' Churchill said three months after the Fulton speech, 'that in a year the Soviets would have been able to do themselves so much harm and chill so many friendships in the English-speaking world.'

In the 'cold war' against Communism Churchill found again the picturesque turn of phrase that had fired the minds of the British people in the 'hot war' against Nazism and Fascism. Communist agents, he warned them, were at work in every country, more insidious than Hitler's 'Fifth Column'. His audiences were readier to believe what he said about Russian Communism than what he had been saying since the war about British Socialism.

It was natural, after the Fulton speech, that Churchill should press for a United States of Europe. He told the Swiss people in Zurich in September 1946, that the countries west of the Iron Curtain should band together to safeguard one another from a return to the Dark Ages, and boldly proposed a partnership between France and Germany as the first step. Those who followed Churchill's lead eagerly during the next two years, and elected him honorary president of the Council of Europe at the Hague in 1948, were surprised and disappointed when, a year later, at Strasbourg, he seemed to have lost all his keenness for his own idea of a united Europe. Only the partnership of France and Germany, which he had suggested at Zurich, seemed to interest him now. Perhaps this was because there was not much enthusiasm in Britain for closer links with the Continent, and an election was shortly to be held.

In 1950 Churchill proposed the arming of Germany for her own defence against the Communist countries. He was accused of mischief-making, as he had been after the Fulton speech, but he boldly reminded his critics that the view he had expressed at Fulton was now commonly held in America and by both the big political parties in England. He warned Parliament that in another war Europe would be communized, and that anti-Communists, whose names were already on Communist lists, would be liquidated. The people listened more gravely now, and his Conservative colleagues were no longer embarrassed by his speeches. His own bitter comment on the 1945 election, that he had been 'dismissed by the British electorate from all further conduct of their affairs', was to be proved inexact.

The Labour Government won the election of 1950 with a sickly majority, and stayed in power just long enough to take the iron and steel industry out of the hands of private owners and give it to the state. In the dreary election campaign of the following year, neither party had many shining promises to make; the Conservatives spoke of the dangers of nationalizing industries, and the Labour speakers condemned Churchill as a warmonger. The Conservatives having won by the narrow margin of twenty-five seats, Churchill became Prime Minister for the second time on 26th October 1951, in the middle of a grave financial crisis.

When it was announced that Churchill and his Foreign Secretary, Eden, were to visit Washington, many people were afraid that they were going 'cap in hand' to ask our wealthy friends for a loan. They returned with an American offer of a million tons of steel for our arms programme, but they had given what amounted to a promise of British help if full-scale war should break out between Communist China and America. Labour M.P.s charged them with risking a world war. Triumphantly Churchill produced documents, like rabbits out of a hat, to show that the Labour Government had secretly given America a similar promise, and that they had also spent scores of millions on plant for an atomic bomb. How could they call *him* a warmonger!

Early the next year the Prime Minister had to announce the death of King George VI to the House of Commons. In the evening he broadcast a tribute to the King's fine qualities as a man and a monarch, and to his fortitude in suffering. He was at London Airport the next day to meet the new Queen, who had learned of her father's death during a tour of Central Africa.

1953 was a year of glittering pageantry and honours for Churchill. The Knighthood of the Garter was conferred on him in April; he was one of the most illustrious and popular figures at the Coronation ceremony in June; and in October he was awarded the Nobel Prize for Literature. But it was also a year of severe shocks to his health and his hopes.

After taking part in the Coronation procession and the ceremony in Westminster Abbey, he added his profession of loyalty to those of the Commonwealth Prime Ministers in a B.B.C. broadcast the same evening, and introduced the Queen's address to her peoples. For the next week he worked at a pace that would have severely taxed most men half his age. To the chairmanship of the Commonwealth Conference of Prime Ministers and the regular duties of a Prime Minister were added those of the Foreign Secretary, for Eden was convalescent after a serious operation. An Anglo-American conference in Bermuda, aimed at easing tension between Russia and the West, was only a month ahead.

It was suddenly announced on 27th June that Sir Winston was to take a month's rest on the advice of his doctors. We know now that he had suffered a 'stroke', with partial paralysis, but so great was his vitality and toughness, even in his seventy-ninth year, that after recuperating at Chartwell he was able to accept the Queen's invitation to the St. Leger in September and to stay with the Royal Family at Balmoral Castle before travelling to the villa near Nice, in the south of France, of his old friend Lord Beaverbrook.

The world had placed great hopes in the Bermuda meeting, for the Russian leader Stalin was dead, and in America Eisenhower, Sir Winston's wartime friend and comrade, had been elected President. Unfortunately for these hopes, an unscrupulous politician in the United States, Senator McCarthy, had caused a nation-wide panic by falsely claiming to have evidence of a Communist spy system permeating the American nation and its Government. No one, not even the President, dared show any 'softening' towards Russia.

During Sir Winston's illness Lord Salisbury talked with President Eisenhower in Washington, but did not persuade him to meet the Russians. At the end of the following June Sir Winston and Eden visited Washington, and found Eisenhower much less hostile to the idea of a 'summit' meeting than his public, but still determined to tread warily.

Churchill again set the world on the alert at a press conference during this visit by proclaiming a new shift in attitude towards Russia. There was a need, he said, to strive for 'peaceful co-existence'. Russia might be 'softened' by cultural contacts between her people and ours which would make them envious of the Western way of life. Eisenhower himself took up the 'peaceful co-existence' slogan, which marked as clear a change of mood as the 'iron curtain' metaphor of the Fulton speech had done eight years earlier.

The hopeful year of 1954 was fittingly rounded off by the celebration of Sir Winston's eightieth birthday. A birthday fund was instituted, to which contributions came from all over the world. Heads of States sent congratulations and presents. On the evening of 30th November Sir Winston and Lady Churchill were the guests of the Lords and Commons in Westminster Hall. The strains of 'Land of Hope and Glory' ushered them to their seats between the Lord Chancellor and the Speaker of the Commons. The leader of the Opposition, Mr. Attlee, presented to Sir Winston a portrait by the celebrated artist Graham Sutherland. The veteran Prime Minister replied to the speeches and presentations with that felicity of phrase which has never deserted him.

When the nation had almost stopped speculating on the date of Sir Winston's retirement, the announcement came in a way that must have won a chuckle from the man who had edited the ultra-Conservative *British Gazette* in the strike-bound Fleet Street of 1926. The only newspaper to announce the event was the Communist *Daily Worker*. The other papers had stopped publication because of a strike of newspapermen!

Sir Winston made his last replies as Prime Minister in Parliament on 31st March 1955. There was an occasion four days later which, like the birthday celebration in Westminster Hall, was without parallel in history; the Queen was Sir Winston's guest at dinner at 10 Downing Street, and proposed the health of her Prime Minister. The following day he offered his resignation at Buckingham Palace, and on 6th May, having been succeeded by Sir Anthony Eden, he left Downing Street for Chartwell. He set out for Syracuse, in Sicily, a few days later to enjoy his first holiday as a private citizen since his appointment as First Lord at the beginning of the war.

The world continued to bestow its rarest honours on the man commonly acknowledged to be 'the greatest living Englishman'—a gold medallion from President Eisenhower in recognition of his services to the free world, the Croix de la Libération from the hands of President de Gaulle, the Charlemagne Peace Prize—but, conscious that his ideal of peaceful co-existence had not been realized, the octogenarian who had saved the world in his seventies toiled on.

Less famous men than Churchill had warned the nation again and again that Russia was making giant strides in scientific and technical education, but very few ordinary people had shown much concern. It was only when the constituents of Woodford heard the long-familiar voice of their M.P. telling them that we were being left behind at a frightening rate that they, and the rest of the western world, sat up and listened. A trust was set up in 1950, headed by Sir Winston, for the building of a men's college at Cambridge to increase our output of scientists and technologists.

A year after he retired, Sir Winston put forward a suggestion of startling boldness—that Russia should be invited to join N.A.T.O., an organization that had seemed to be an alliance of Russia's enemies. It must have been a bitter moment for Churchill when the German Foreign Minister poured cold water on his idea by saying that it was too soon to talk of a new Russia.

The four volumes of *A History of the English-Speaking Peoples* were published between 1956 and 1958. Some critics complained that history as a story of kings, nobles and battles was out of date; but the narrative is no less fluent and exciting, the rolling phrases no less majestic, than in earlier Churchillian history.

Sir Winston was gravely ill in Monte Carlo in 1958 with pneumonia, the same illness that he had barely allowed to interrupt his herculean work at the time of the great war-time conferences; but he fought back so strongly that he was able to tell his Woodford constituents a year later that he would stand for Parliament at the next general election, and to address the House of Commons on the occasion of his eighty-fifth birthday. A fall in November 1960, in which he broke a small bone in his back, caused him a few weeks' inactivity, but he is again satisfying his lifelong desire for travel and change, dividing his time between Chartwell, the French Riviera and cruises in the yacht of his friend Aristotle Onassis, the Greek shipowner. He is now savouring the leisure largely denied to him throughout a phenomenally busy life.

This is the end of a very short account of activities so many and varied that they might provide the raw material for half a dozen very different life stories. Sir Winston has been soldier, war correspondent, novelist, biographer, editor and statesman, and has miraculously found time for painting, building, farming, racehorse-owning and the duties of a father. He has served as a soldier in four continents, and as a Member of Parliament in six reigns. He has piloted reforms through Parliament which have made life easier for millions of working people; and he has ordered troops into action against workers made rebellious by hardship. At different times he has been the most popular and the most hated man in Britain among those same working people. He loves comfort and good living, yet he is physically robust and tough; he has loved war and fighting, yet he has often been moved to tears by the suffering that war brings; he was undistinguished, even dull, as a schoolboy, but his adult career has been spectacular and brilliant.

This variety, and these contradictions, may partly be explained by the uncommon background against which his life has been lived, and by his uncommon view of life and his role in it. The son of an outstanding Minister of Victoria's reign, born in Blenheim Palace, the home of the great first Duke of Marlborough, and breathing the atmosphere of greatness from his earliest years, he never doubted that he too had been chosen for greatness. With this faith and his tremendous energy, he grasped at every chance of distinction, and usually achieved it.

That is why he has been criticized for seeing himself, and talking and writing of himself, as the hero of a series of adventure stories. That is why he has been accused of imagining enemies and causes for quarrels, and of behaving in such a way as to create real enemies and real quarrels. Even his warmest admirers cannot claim that he has never been guilty of these faults; but even his sternest critics must be sorry that so few people in the thirties listened to his warnings of future disaster, and they must be glad that he was there to play his truly heroic part in the grimly real struggle of the Second World War.

Glossary

rain, on 1st April. A few days after this date, the
Chancellor announces the details of his Budget to the
House of Commons. A debate follows, the result of
which is the passing of the ....
Budget the Act is passed
its way. When a bill of the House of Commons
....

Act: A law made by Parliament. Only Parliament itself
can change or abolish an Act of Parliament.

Admiralty: The *Ministry* which controls the Royal
Navy. (See also *First Lord* and *First Sea Lord*.)

Armistice: A truce, usually to give nations at war a
chance to arrange a peace treaty. The Armistice of 1918
was to last for thirty days, but a permanent peace was
decided on during that time. The Second World War
ended in the *unconditional surrender* of the Germans and
Japanese, and so there was no armistice.

Battalion: See *Division*.

Board of Trade: The *Ministry* which has some control
over the materials and planning of industry in Britain,
the sale of British goods abroad, and our merchant
shipping.

Bolsheviks: The most powerful of many revolutionary
groups in Russia, the Bolsheviks took control of the
Revolution of 1917.

Brigade: See *Division*.

Budget: Each autumn, all government departments
calculate how much money they are likely to need during the next financial year. They then put the results of
their calculations before the Chancellor of the Exchequer, the Minister in charge of the nation's finances.
This bill, and the taxes that the Chancellor decides are
necessary to pay it, form the Budget. The financial year

starts on 1st April. A few days after this date, the Chancellor announces the details of his Budget to the House of Commons. A debate follows, the result of which is the Finance Act. The new taxes become law when the Act is passed.

BY-ELECTION: When a Member of the *House of Commons* retires, becomes a Member of the *House of Lords* or dies, a by-election is held in his *constituency* to choose his successor.

CABINET: A small group of ministers which decides the policy of the Government under the chairmanship of the Prime Minister.

CANDIDATE: A person who presents himself for election to Parliament.

CHANCELLOR OF THE EXCHEQUER: See *Budget*.

CHANCELLOR (OF GERMANY): He corresponds to our Prime Minister, though Hitler made himself a dictator when he became Chancellor.

COALITION GOVERNMENT: A government formed by two or more parties which agree to work together. This may happen (*a*) because none of the parties has won enough seats to govern alone, or (*b*) because party rivalry must be set aside, either in wartime or during a peacetime crisis like the depression of 1929.

COMMISSION: Authority granted to army officers by the sovereign, and to naval officers by the *Lords of the Admiralty*, to carry out their duties.

COMMUNISM: A political creed which holds that all property should belong to the community, and that each person should be given what he needs as payment for his work. (See also *Socialism*.)

CONSERVATIVE PARTY: The party which has formed the Government or the *Opposition* ever since the early nineteenth century. It is against revolutionary changes in the system of government and the way of life of the nation.

CONSTITUENCY, CONSTITUENTS: An M.P.'s constituents are the voters who live in his constituency, the area he represents in Parliament.

CONSTITUTION: The broad principles, such as freedom of speech and the right to vote, by which a country is governed.

CONSULATES: Offices which a government maintains in important foreign cities to help and protect its own people while they are abroad.

DIVISION: There are three infantry battalions in a brigade, and three brigades in a division. Besides infantry, a division has artillery, engineer, medical, ordnance, service and signal units.

ELECTORATE: The voters of a nation as a whole.

FASCISM: A political creed which allows only one party, and directs all the energies and patriotism of the people to the service and glory of the state. It is opposed to *Communism*.

FIRST LORD OF THE ADMIRALTY: The Cabinet Minister who is responsible to Parliament for naval affairs.

FIRST SEA LORD: The Admiral who is the *First Lord's* chief naval expert.

FLEET AIR ARM: Originally a detachment of the R.A.F. which worked with the navy from 1924, the Fleet Air Arm became the air branch of the Royal Navy in 1938.

FOREIGN OFFICE: The Ministry headed by the Secretary of State for Foreign Affairs, or Foreign Secretary. Besides its establishment in London dealing with foreign affairs, it controls British embassies, consulates and legations abroad.

GENERAL ELECTION: After a Parliament has been dissolved, the election of a new Parliament consisting of the 625 Members of the House of Commons who represent all the *constituencies* of England, Scotland, Wales and Northern Ireland.

HOME OFFICE: The Ministry responsible for law and order within the country. It is headed by the *Home Secretary*.

HOME SECRETARY: The most important Secretary of State. (See also *Home Office*.)

HOUSE OF COMMONS: The assembly of 625 Members of Parliament, chosen by the people, which, with the Sovereign and the House of Lords, forms the British Government. (See also *General Election*.)

HOUSE OF LORDS: An assembly of 26 bishops, about 850 peers and 9 'law lords'. The peers' membership of the House, like their titles, is passed on to their heirs. The law lords are judges, and do not pass on their titles. Bills passed by the House of Commons must afterwards be passed by the House of Lords, but nowadays the Lords cannot prevent such Bills from becoming law.

LABOUR PARTY: The Labour Party is the British *Socialist* party, and came from the *Trade Union* movement in the late nineteenth century. It had only two M.P.s in 1900, but after the First World War it became the official *Opposition* party, and by the twenties it was the largest single party in Parliament.

LEASE-LEND, OR LEND-LEASE: The United States sent war materials and other supplies to Britain and Russia between 1941 and 1945 without payment, on the understanding that those countries would try to send the United States the goods she needed in return. Britain repaid about one-seventh of her debt in this way, but she received a loan of nearly 4,000 million dollars from the United States after the end of Lease-Lend.

LIBERAL PARTY: The opponents of the Conservatives in

the nineteenth century, the Liberals lost ground rapidly to the Labour Party in the twentieth. They wanted social and political progress, but they were not a working-class party.

LINES OF COMMUNICATION: The routes along which an army's forward troops keep in touch with their bases.

METROPOLITAN POLICE: The police force of Greater London.

MINISTER: The member who is responsible to Parliament for the work of an important government department.

MOBILIZATION: Putting the armed forces in a state of readiness for war.

NATIONAL GOVERNMENT: A *Coalition* representing all parties in Parliament during an emergency.

NATIONALIZATION: The taking over by the Government of an important industry that has been run privately before. The coal, gas and electricity industries are among the nationalized industries.

NATIONALIST: A person who wants, and may fight for, his nation's freedom from some other country that controls it.

NATURALIZED: A person of foreign birth who is officially declared a citizen of the country he lives in is said to be naturalized.

NEUTRAL: Neutral countries are those that do not take sides in a war.

OPPOSITION: The Opposition party is the second largest party in Parliament, and opposes the policy of the Government.

PACIFIST: A person who believes that it is wrong to use force in settling a quarrel, and is therefore opposed to war.

'PEACEFUL CO-EXISTENCE': An agreement to 'live and let live' between nations that dislike each other's forms of government and ways of life, like the United States and Russia.

POLLS: The voting, or the places where people vote, during an election.

PRESIDENT OF THE BOARD OF TRADE: See *Board of Trade*.

SOCIALISM: The most extreme Socialist, the Communist, believes that all property should belong to the state. Milder Socialists believe that the state should own, plan and control only those industries that provide us with the goods and services we cannot do without. (See also *Communism* and *Labour Party*.)

SPEAKER: The chairman of the House of Commons.

'SPHERES OF INFLUENCE': Parts of Europe over which the nations that won the war were to have some control.

STRATEGY: The planning and control of a military campaign or a war, including the placing and movements of large forces.

TACTICS: The control, placing and movement of troops in a battle.

TRADE UNION: A workers' organization in an industry or group of industries. A trade union tries to get more pay, shorter hours of work and better conditions for its members.

UNCONDITIONAL SURRENDER: If a country at war agrees to lay down its arms on *condition* that its enemies allow it, for example, to keep some territory it has conquered, that is a *conditional* surrender. If a country is so thoroughly beaten that it has to surrender without asking any favours, that is an *un*conditional surrender.

UNEMPLOYMENT INSURANCE: A system by which a worker regularly pays small sums of money to the Government, and receives payments from the Government when he is out of work.

Reading List

THE HISTORICAL BACKGROUND

A History of English Life, Political and Social (3rd edition, 1953). Amabel Williams-Ellis and F. J. Fisher. Methuen. (Especially Volume IV, Parts III and IV.)

The Day before Yesterday. Noel Streatfeild. Collins.

Six Great Englishmen. Aubrey de Selincourt. Hamish Hamilton. (Has chapters on Marlborough and Winston Churchill.)

People in History. R. J. Unstead. A. & C. Black. (Chapter 33 on John and Sarah Churchill.)

THE SUDAN CAMPAIGN AND THE BOER WAR

Opening Africa. L. F. Hobley. Methuen.

With Gordon in the Sudan. Anne Tibble. Muller. (Especially chapters 6–9.)

THE FIRST WORLD WAR

The True Book about the First World War. A. H. Booth. Muller.

From Kitty Hawk to Outer Space—The Story of the Aeroplane. L. E. Snellgrove. Longmans.

THE SECOND WORLD WAR

The Second World War. Winston S. Churchill. School edition compiled by Andrew Scotland. Cassell.

The True Book about the Second World War. A. Farrer Hockley. Muller.

Victory at Sea, 1939–1945. Lieut.-Commander P. K. Kemp. Muller.

Valiant Occasions. J. E. Macdonell. Constable. (*Prince of Wales, Repulse, Graf Spee*.)

From Kitty Hawk to Outer Space. L. E. Snellgrove. Longmans.

The Summer of Dunkirk by Arthur Bryant, and *The Great Miracle* by Edward Shanks. Kemsley House.

The Battle of Britain by Arthur Bryant, and *The Few* by Edward Shanks. Kemsley House.

(The last two consist of articles and poems reprinted from the *Daily Sketch* and presented in booklet form to the libraries of British public and secondary schools.)

Twentieth Century Cavalcade. H. Bellis. Hutchinson. (Chapter VI on Franklin D. Roosevelt.)

PARLIAMENT AND POLITICS

Parliament. K. Mackenzie. Methuen.

State and People. J. O. Murray. Harrap. (Part II: Central Government.)

Twentieth Century Cavalcade. H. Bellis. Hutchinson. (Chapter V on David Lloyd George.)

Index

INDEX

INDEX